George Herbert Bartlett

A commercial Trip with an uncommercial Ending

George Herbert Bartlett

A commercial Trip with an uncommercial Ending

ISBN/EAN: 9783337146351

Printed in Europe, USA, Canada, Australia, Japan

Cover: Foto ©ninafisch / pixelio.de

More available books at **www.hansebooks.com**

A Commercial Trip with an Uncommercial Ending

G. H. BARTLETT

Positively the Greatest Discovery of the Age.

VAN BUREN'S
Rheumatic Compound

IS WARRANTED TO CURE THE WORST CASES OF

RHEUMATISM.

INFLAMMATORY,
SCIATICA,
CHRONIC,
GOUT,
TIC-DOULOUREUX,
NEURALGIA,
And all this class of Diseases.

VAN BUREN'S
A
Positive Cure
FOR
RHEUMATISM.
Rheumatic Compound.

Being a BLOOD PURIFIER, and acting direct on the bowels, as well as the nervous system, and liver, it naturally relieves

HEADACHES,
INDIGESTION,
PALPITATION,
HEART DISEASE
And all diseases arising from a
Disordered Stomach.

This Article is Purely Vegetable, contains no Minerals.

PRICE, 50 CENTS AND $1.00 PER BOTTLE.

Liberal Discount to the Trade.

B. VAN BUREN, Chemist and Druggist,

MANUFACTURER AND PROPRIETOR,

1249 WEST MADISON STREET,

CHICAGO.

FOR SALE BY DRUGGISTS GENERALLY

Press Notices of "A Commercial Trip."

How one of the firm was sent out in place of an experienced commercial traveler to Pittsburg, Columbus, Cincinnati, and other large cities in the West, how he succeeded in getting orders, and what came of his trip, is effectively told in this narrative. The sleeping car, the hotel, and the houses called upon, furnish very laughable scenes, which are brightly and humorously described. * * * * Wit flows freely, and sparkles on every page, although the incidents were enough to cause boisterous mirth. It is very cleverly done.—*Boston Globe.*

A story, bright and pleasant throughout. * * *
—New Orleans *Times-Democrat.*

* * * * Mr. Bartlett writes pleasantly, and his work has the merit of pretty faithfully reflecting a phase of contemporary life.—*N. Y. Commercial.*

* * * * An amusing account of the adventures of a young man devoted to his violin and fishing, who started out on his first commercial trip and fell in love on the way. His experiences in hotels, boats and steam cars were very absurd, and are cleverly described. It is generally considered a dangerous thing to attempt to write a funny book, but the author of this odd little volume may be congratulated at having made so much of a success.—*Milwaukee Sentinel.*

A story of a purely American character, full of amusing incident. Hotel and railway adventures, various mishaps and misapprehensions, offer excellent material, which is brightly and humorously treated.—*N. Y. Journal.*

One may be a highly successful business man in the conducting of an establishment, and yet prove an unsuccessful commercial traveler, even for his own house. In a pretty little book entitled "A Commercial Trip with an Uncommercial Ending," George H. Bartlett relates in a very racy and readable style, the experience of Mr. Clark, of the New York firm of Dale & Clark, who took a commercial trip to relieve their faithful commercial traveler, Morgan, who had become considerably run down and needed a vacation. * * * * Clark soon found that commercial traveling was not recreative work, neither was it work that anybody could easily accomplish. His encounters with swarms of agents of rival houses, and experience with buyers, are graphically related. * * * * —*Home Journal*, Boston.

* * * * The account of the woman bargaining for the sleeping berth at Pittsburg is especially good.—*N. Y. World*.

A racy little romance, the general character of which will be at once surmised by the title. * * * * The romance is pleasantly woven through the business transactions of the commercial traveler, and the story will make agreeable summer reading.—*Troy Times*.

* * * * Told in a witty and vivacious style.—*Times-Star*, Cincinnati.

It is natural, with genuine humor. The very simplicity of the little sketches are their chief charm. * * * —St. John's (N. B.) *Globe*.

RAND, McNALLY & CO., Publishers, 148-154 Monroe St., Chicago.

A Commercial Trip

WITH

AN UNCOMMERCIAL ENDING

BY

GEORGE H. BARTLETT

RAND, McNALLY & CO.,
148 TO 154 MONROE STREET, CHICAGO.
323 BROADWAY, NEW YORK.

COPYRIGHT BY
GEORGE H. BARTLETT
1884.

A COMMERCIAL TRIP WITH AN UNCOMMERCIAL ENDING.

I.

"Office of Dale and Clark,
"New York, Aug. 28, 188–.

"Dear Clark:
"Morgan is a good deal run down from travelling so much during the hot weather. He expects to start on another trip next Tuesday, but he really needs rest, and ought to take a vacation. Cannot you make the trip in his place? Perhaps you will think there is no good reason why I should not go myself—but please to remember that I have a family, while you are a bachelor! The following would be your route:—Pittsburgh, Columbus, Cincinnati, Louisville, Indianapolis, Terre Haute, St. Louis, Chicago, Milwaukee, Detroit, Toledo, and Cleveland. It would take you about four weeks to cover the ground. Please let me know at once whether you will go."

Clark was aboard his yacht, the *Fleetwing*, anchored in New London Harbor for the night, when this letter was received from his partner. In company with three other young bachelors he was taking a cruise through Long Island Sound. They had spent the past few days trolling for bluefish, which they had found very abundant between Little Gull Light-house and Fisher's Island. The letter had arrived toward the close of the two weeks set apart for the cruise, so their rovings were not much shortened by Clark's decision to sail for New York on the following morning. The *Fleetwing* made a quick run to New York, and Clark was again at his office attending to business. He had seen the *Fleetwing* sail away with Morgan and several friends on board, Clark having persuaded the traveller to take a cruise.

Tuesday afternoon Clark was at his bachelor quarters, packing. He had taken Morgan's trunk, which was of moderate size and constructed in a most substantial manner. In truth, it had so much iron about it that it bore some resemblance to a safe. This trunk had been in active service for ten years, and baggagemen had become discouraged by its obstinate tenacity, and given up all hopes of ever being able to do it any serious damage.

The few samples which Clark was obliged to carry were fastened upon cards, taking up but little space in the trunk. Most of the goods in which the firm dealt were staple articles, and it was not necessary to carry samples of these. In one tray of the trunk Clark had carefully packed a case containing a great treasure—namely, an old and valuable violin. It had the sweetest of voices, and Clark had played upon it ever since he was ten years old.

The packing being finished, Clark locked the trunk, having, however, first taken a farewell look at his violin, and saying: "Good-bye, old friend, till we meet in Pittsburgh." Then he packed his valise, after which, as it still lacked an hour before the hack would call to take him to the depôt, he unlocked his trunk, took out his violin, and stood before a small picture. It was an oil-painting by Meyer von Bremem—the subject being a sleeping child, while three other children stood gazing lovingly upon the little sleeper, the faces of all being lighted up by a candle held by one of the children. It was a very beautiful and life-like picture, and Clark had become very much attached to the little group. His intimate friends usually spoke of the painting as "Clark's children," and the violin went by the name of "Clark's wife." There were some who wondered whether the constant presence of an "old bow," paying Clark's wife so much attention, ever made trouble in the family; while others, when this was hinted, would say contemptuously, "Fiddlesticks!"

After Clark had stood for a few moments, gazing fatherly upon his children, a voice came from the violin like unto that of a little child singing a nursery hymn. Then it seemed as though other children's voices joined in, so sweet was the harmony which came from the instrument.

II.

IT did not appear very inviting to Clark when he entered the sleeping-car at Jersey City. The weather was warm and the air in the Pullman hot and close. Another circumstance which did not portend comfort and a good night's rest was the presence of a family in which were two fretful children and a crying infant. The father and mother were doing their best to quiet their little ones, but met with no success. Some of the passengers showed bad temper and worse manners by turning around and frowning continually upon the children and parents.

The family had been obliged to take upper berths, having come after all the lowers had been engaged. Now, the thought of the mother occupying an upper berth with a little baby made Clark feel uneasy; for, he reasoned, should either fall from that "second story," severe injury might be the result. He soon offered to give up his lower berth and in exchange take one of the uppers, and was warmly thanked for his thoughtfulness.

When the time arrived for him to ascend into his elevated bed, it seemed to him a little like climbing up a tree for a nap, *à la* Robinson Crusoe.

He had been asleep for an hour or so when he awoke and was conscious of breathing bad air. Every berth was occupied; and the proper ventilation of a well-filled sleeping-car is one thing which inventors have not yet solved.

Clark sat up, put his head out from between the curtains of his berth and looked for the colored porter, intending to request that a door or window be opened. The porter was discovered on the floor, at the further end of the car, fast asleep.

Clark thought: "I can't awake him at this distance without disturbing some of the sleeping passengers. I might throw a shoe at him and attract him in that way; but unfortunately I shall have to slide down this tree to get one. I'll open a door or window myself."

He partially dressed, descended from his lofty bed, walked softly to one end of the car, and opened the door. This let in too great a rush of air and cinders, so he shut it and tried to raise a window. It would not budge. He tried another with the same result. Then he went softly to the other end of the car and succeeded there in opening a window. The cool mountain air was very refreshing, and Clark sat there for some time, nearly falling asleep. When he started to return to his berth he could not, for the life of him, remember just where it was located. He knew it was near the centre of the car, but on which side? He tried to locate his berth by his hat, which he had hung on the outside, but there were a number of hats which looked just alike, any one of which might be his.

"If I could only see the inside of these hats I could tell mine by the manufacturer's brand. Or, I can find my berth by drawing aside curtains, for mine will be empty; but I shall then run a risk of peeping into other persons' beds. I'll try investigating hats."

Being tall he had no difficulty in reaching to where the hats hung. The first one he examined was new, like his own, and had the right maker's name inside.

"Hit it the first time!" he said to himself, and then proceeded to climb up.

"What in thunder are you doing?" fairly roared a gruff voice as Clark partially entered what proved to be an occupied berth.

"Beg your pardon. I'm mistaken," said Clark.

"You are! and by a big majority! I have a pistol under my pillow for fellows who make such *mistakes*. You got off cheap."

"I'll try *on* the next hat," thought Clark. "I never saw so many new hats together outside of a hat store, and they are all enough alike to be brothers. A woman could tell her hat among a thousand, but alas! for poor man!"

Clark was going softly about and was on the point of reaching for another hat when he observed the porter was watching him.

"I 'se seen yer! I 'se seen yer!" cried the porter, throwing aside a blanket and standing up.

"I wish you would tell me where my berth is," said Clark.

"That's the way with these car-thieves. They are always hunting for their berths. It's an old game," said a voice which Clark recognized as belonging to the man who slept with a pistol under his pillow.

Clark was angry now and said:

"If any one wishes to call me a thief let him come down *here!*"

By this time the passengers were pretty generally awake; numerous heads appeared from behind the curtains, and all eyes were fixed upon the car-thief. Clark was amused as well as angry now—a rather unusual combination.

"I tell you I have lost my berth," he said.

"Advertise for it in the *New York Herald*," cried one.

"Where was it last seen by you?" inquired another.

"Did you drop it in the car or lose it crossing the ferry?"

"Is it gentle and kind, or will it bite?"

"What color was it?"

"What reward do you offer?"

"Are you sure you did not pawn it?"

These and other questions were put in rapid succession by several young men whom Clark took to be commercial travellers, and who evidently saw only the comical side of the loss of a berth.

"What is your number?" inquired the porter, when the other cross-examiners had given him a chance to ask the question.

"I don't know. I exchanged my original berth, which was lower eight, for an upper near the centre of the car."

By this time, many of the passengers being thoroughly convinced that a car-thief had been going the rounds, now began examining their pockets, etc. Those who had secreted valuables under mattresses or elsewhere, were not satisfied until they had taken an inventory of their goods and chattels. In their zeal to discover whether or not they had been robbed, pillows were overturned and came tumbling down, and there was much commotion and loud talking. The children and infant soon started on their crying way, and Clark was greatly exasperated upon hearing the mother remark that "she would never have taken him for a thief, he looked so honest!"

One man said the proper way to treat car-thieves was to lynch them on the spot, and that the bell-rope would be just the thing to do it with!

Several voices cried, "That's so!"

Clark was laughing now in spite of the unpleasantness of the whole affair. The porter found the lost berth, and assured the passengers that "The gentleman was all right." Quiet reigned again, and Clark slept some after this; but he was glad when day dawned. Soon after seven o'clock the black smoke, which hovers over Pittsburgh, came in view, and half an hour later Pittsburgh itself.

After a good breakfast at the hotel Clark went to his room, opened his trunk, and took therefrom his violin. He soon played himself into a happy frame of mind, and then prepared for business.

III.

THE firm of which Clark was a partner represented certain well-known manufacturing companies. All sales were made through Dale & Clark, that firm disposing of the entire product of the mills, and selling almost exclusively to the wholesale trade.

It might give Clark's trip a personal aspect did we state the line of goods handled by him, so we will give fictitious names to the articles to be sold, for the goods must have names, otherwise Clark will not be able to transact business satisfactorily. The staples we will call hulls, masts, stays, booms, and jibs, and the articles of which he carried samples, keels. It will be noticed that these names are of a nautical turn, but it should be remembered that Clark was an enthusiastic yachtsman, and it is right that his tastes should be consulted in this christening. Besides, the names are appropriate from the fact that he felt all at sea in the rôle of commercial traveller, for it was to be his first experience in that line.

Each particular pattern of keel had a number to designate it, and, as before stated, the samples were fastened to cards, the whole making only a moderate package.

When Clark started out that morning to call upon the wholesale firms, he carried the samples of keels with him.

Before leaving the hotel, he had gone to the office to borrow or hire an umbrella, for to him there was every indication that there was to be a heavy fall of rain soon.

"What in the world do you want with an umbrella?" inquired the clerk.

"It is as black as ink out; looks as though we were going to have a thunder-storm," said Clark.

"Thunder-storm! Why, you forget you are in the 'Smoky City.' This is a clear day for us."

Clark's first call was upon one of the leading Pittsburgh firms, and he received a pleasant welcome. The buyer asked to be excused for a short time, in order that he might look over the morning's mail. While Clark was waiting, another traveller came in, and another, and still another, and " still they came," until seven representatives of firms dealing in similar goods were in the store. The buyer introduced Clark to each and all of them. Now, for seven men to be assembled in one store for the purpose of selling to one man seemed to Clark to be a little overdoing matters. He thought:

"I never knew before that salesmen ran in 'schools,' like blue-fish."

There was a lively conversation kept up, with not a few short stories, while the buyer was engaged with the mail. The travellers were evidently well acquainted with each other, and entirely at home in that store. Instead of having come there as competitors, it seemed more like a meeting of old friends for the purpose of having a friendly chat and an interchange of laughable anecdotes.

Having finished with the mail, the buyer—who was also senior member of the firm—joined the party and said: "Well, gentlemen, I don't see but that I am unusually favored this morning. This is a regular ovation. The only difficulty will be to make my order go around. It will require a miracle, for what would it be among so many?"

"Let's draw lots!" suggested one traveller.

"Any way which suits you, gentlemen," said the buyer.

"You might issue tickets as they do in barber shops, letting each take his turn."

"And then get shaved!" said the buyer.

"Oh!" came in chorus.

"Suppose we sing 'Buy and Buy' as appropriate to the occasion."

This suggestion, which came from Clark, called forth another "Oh!" from the travellers.

It was not long before one salesman after another dropped out, first making an appointment to call later in the day, and Clark was left alone with the buyer. After some conversation not of a business character, Clark came to the conclusion that the buyer expected him to "open fire" on the topic of goods and prices.

Clark had a limited experience as a salesman at home, but there it was the buyer who approached the salesman. Now that the tables were turned Clark scarcely knew how to begin operations.

As a commencement he asked: "By the way, what is the state of your stock at the present time?"

"Pretty comfortable, thank you; how is yours?" replied the buyer, smilingly.

"So as to be about!" said Clark.

"All right. Give us some prices."

"Hulls are worth twenty-two cents," said Clark.

"That's news! I have n't paid certain of your competitors over twenty cents for some time."

"Then you have been buying goods that are inferior to ours. You know our hulls are much superior to the general run."

"That's the case with everybody's. 'T is like the railroad maps and circulars gotten up by the respective lines: Each road has the safest and smoothest track, is the shortest, makes the best time, has the finest scenery, etc."

The buyer did not say this in a disagreeable manner, but nevertheless he made Clark feel uncomfortable.

"You will admit, I suppose, that our brand of hulls is of first-rate quality?" queried Clark.

"Of course I will. But there are others

which we can buy for less and sell for just as much. That's the story in a nutshell."

"Then I can't sell you any hulls?"

"Not at that price."

"How are you stocked on jibs?"

"You can't touch me on those. I'm full."

"And masts?"

"Could buy a lot at a special low price."

"Well, how does twelve cents seem to you?"

"Not as low as eleven."

"I cannot sell you at better than twelve, and, to the best of my knowledge and belief, that is as low as you can buy them anywhere."

"Very well, we will not dispute on that point. I can't pay you over eleven cents."

"Then I can't sell you any masts," said Clark.

Clark now proposed showing his samples of keels, and the buyer expressed a willingness to look at them.

"What is the price of 28?"

"One twenty-five."

"I would like to show you one of the same size and pattern which I bought at one fifteen from Dickenson."

"You must know that Dickenson's keels are trash."

"They sell well."

"Yes, very likely. But that is n't the point. The goods are miserably made."

"All we can afford to consider is the difference between the price at which we buy and the price at which we sell. We are doing business for profit, not for glory."

Clark found he was not getting on well with this buyer, and he finally lost his temper.

"When we have any thing mean and cheap to offer you we will mail quotations," said Clark.

The buyer replied: "Oh, don't trouble yourself to do so."

Clark could not help feeling disturbed by this, his first experience, as a commercial traveller. Here was a firm which had been dealing with Dale & Clark for years, and yet Clark, instead of obtaining an order, had simply succeeded in antagonizing the buyer. Clark could not believe that the man was so unreasonable as to expect to buy superior goods at the same prices as common goods. Dickenson's keels were of an entirely different grade from Clark's, and every one at all posted knew that to be the case.

"I fear I showed no tact," thought Clark, as he considered the matter. "I was undoubtedly too ready to assert, and even dispute. I should have kept cool and used my persuasive powers, if I have any."

He made another call; but as the buyer was already engaged with a salesman, he merely introduced himself and said he would call on the morrow. He met with a like experience at another house, and still another, until this hunting for orders seemed to him a good deal like looking for a needle in a hay-mow. He did no business that day. "Fishing for orders is n't to be compared to blue-fishing," he thought. "The fish are either on some other fellow's hook or else they will not bite at mine."

IV.

WHEN Clark awoke the following morning it was pretty dark, though the sun had been up over an hour.

He found innumerable black specks floating in his water-pitcher, and a white shirt, in which he had placed studs the night before, and left upon a chair, bosom upward, was also covered with the same description of blackness.

Clark had, as usual, left a window wide open, and the soot had rained in and covered every thing.

Now had he been a Pittsburgher, he would, upon discovering those black specks upon his shirt-bosom, simply have blown or shaken them off. What he *did* do was this : he took a towel and attempted to brush them off. Many long, black streaks was the consequence.

" My bosom is in mourning!" he exclaimed, as he discarded the shirt and studded another.

After breakfast, as it was still too early for

business calls, Clark thought it would be pleasant to cross the bridge which spans the Monongahela River near the hotel, and ride up to the top of the bluffs on an inclined-plane railway which he could see in operation from the hotel.

"It is a dark day. I can hardly believe this is nothing but smoke and soot; but perhaps it is. I will not again display my greenness by asking for an umbrella."

Thus thought Clark as he stepped out upon the sidewalk. When part way over the bridge he stood looking down into the water, and received a dose of black smoke from a passing steamer's smoke-stack.

"How soon the white sails of the *Fleetwing* would turn black here. If I was out sailing on the Sound and saw as black a sky as this, I would either shorten sail or make for a harbor, double quick. One of Pittsburgh's mock thunder-storms."

He had ceased soliloquizing, and was walking slowly on when a pouring rain set in. The wind blew great guns too. The bridge was not a covered one, and Clark ran at his best speed all the way back to the hotel, and stood before the clerk in the office pretty wet. It was the same clerk who had smiled when Clark had asked for an umbrella the day before.

"I would like to inquire whether there is any way of judging any thing about the weather here?" said Clark.

"Certainly there is," said the clerk; "if you go out and don't get wet, it is a pleasant day; but if, as in your case this morning, you come back as wet as you are now, you are pretty safe in concluding 't is stormy—that is, unless you have fallen into the river."

"Thank you for the information," said Clark. "I am glad to know how to tell! Can I hire an umbrella?"

"Yes; the boy at the news-stand has them to let."

Clark procured an umbrella and then sallied forth to call upon those dealers with whom he had appointments. His first call that day was upon a very jovial, whole-souled man, the buying partner of one of the solid Pittsburgh firms. Clark had seen him but a moment the day before, but now found him disengaged and ready to hear prices and look at samples of keels.

There was no badgering at all on the part of this buyer. He merely took down the prices quoted, and asked Clark to call again at four o'clock. He also invited Clark to go out to East Liberty to spend the night with him; but as Clark was to leave for Columbus that evening, this invitation had to be declined.

"We get away from the smoky atmosphere out there," said the buyer; "but then we don't mind the smoke much, after all."

"I have not seen the sun since I have been here, and have been thinking it would be a good speculation to go into the balloon business, and charge so much per head for a peep at that luminary," said Clark.

"A very good idea!" said the buyer. "Ah! we glory in our smoke! When the sun shines through it any worth mentioning it is a dark day for us, for it shows business at our mills is dull. Although we are under a cloud most of the time we are as happy as most mortals, I think."

"That probably arises from the fact that you are entirely sooted!" said Clark.

The buyer looked at the perpetrator of this atrocious pun with a glance which seemed to say : " I am sorry if you are given to that kind of thing ! "

Clark saw other firms that day but was not successful in making sales. There were too many travellers in town, Clark thought, and he felt himself at a disadvantage, being a stranger to the buyers. He was undoubtedly too modest in his efforts, and he knew it was largely his own fault that he had not succeeded in obtaining satisfactory interviews with certain of the buyers. In truth, he felt that he had lost orders by default.

At four o'clock he again called upon the buyer who had requested him to do so, and was given several sheets of paper, which contained liberal orders for keels as well as for staples.

V.

WHEN he went to the depôt to secure a berth on the sleeping-car for Columbus, he found a woman standing in front of the Pullman-Car office. She had just commenced asking questions, and the agent was answering her to the best of his ability and with all due patience.

"Are you the man who sells sleeping-car tickets?" asked the woman.

"Yes, madam, I am."

"Does the sleeping-car run through to where I am going?"

"I don't know where that is yet, as you have n't told me."

"To New York. I live there, and have for ten years. Does the sleeping-car run all the way through without change?"

"Yes, madam."

"I 'm glad of that. How much will it cost me for a berth?"

"Two dollars and a half."

"Two dollars and fifty cents?"

"Yes, madam."

"That is very high! Have you a real good berth for me?"

"Yes; you can have either lower six or seven on train leaving Pittsburgh at eight o'clock."

"At eight to-night?"

"Yes, madam."

"How long does it take to go to New York?"

"You will arrive there about ten o'clock to-morrow morning."

"Let me think! When I came out here last month, I left at six in the evening and arrived here about eight the next morning. In what part of the car are the berths you mentioned I could have?"

"Both are near the centre."

"Are they on the same side of the car?"

"No, madam—right opposite."

"I wish I knew which was the best side of the car. Can you tell me?"

"There is not a particle of difference."

"What kind of persons have the berths next to six and seven?—I think you said six and seven; did n't you?"

"I did; but I don't know who will have the adjoining berths."

"Can't you find out?"

"No, madam; I can't."

"I am sorry for that, because I am told all kinds of folks travel on sleeping-cars, and I would like to be next to *genteel* people. There will not be any hard wheels under me; will there? I have been told to get a berth away from the hard wheels. Will there be any under me?"

"No, madam; the wheels are near ends of car."

"What kind of beds are there?"

"Hair mattresses."

"*Hair*, did I understand you to say?"

"Yes, madam."

"O dear me! I prefer feathers—am more used to them."

"The ticket, madam, will be two dollars and a half. Please decide what you will do, for there are several others waiting until you are served."

"Two dollars and fifty cents?"

"Yes."

"One thing I forgot to ask you: Can myself and daughter sleep comfortably in one berth?"

"I think so."

"My daughter Sarah is a pretty large girl. There she sits, over yonder. Nothing extra to pay when two occupy a berth?"

"No, madam."

"And the train leaves when?"

"Eight o'clock."

"To-night, I believe you said?"

"Yes."

"What time have you now?"

"Half-past six."

"Is that railroad time?"

"It is."

"How much did you say it would be?"

"Two dollars and a half."

"Two dollars and fifty cents?"

"Yes, madam."

"That is very, *very* high for a bed. I guess, as 't is n't a feather bed, Sarah and I will sit up. There is a moon to-night, and we can see the mountains by moonlight."

After Clark and the other waiting travellers had secured berths, Clark said to the agent:

"You are the most patient man I ever met."

"You refer to that questioner, I suppose. Well, I try to be polite, but sometimes I lose my temper. Fat men give us lots of trouble when we have nothing left but upper berths. Here comes one now. If he is going West he will have to take an upper, for I'm all sold out of lowers."

Clark stood aside and heard the following dialogue:

"I want a lower berth in centre of car for Cincinnati, leaving at eight to-night."

"I'm very sorry, but we have nothing left but uppers. I can give you an upper in the centre of car."

"I don't want an upper, and won't put up with one. I could n't sleep a wink. You surely would n't expect *me* to climb up into an upper berth."

"Am sorry, but I have nothing else. You will have a step-ladder to assist you."

"I tell you I won't take an upper berth. You are no doubt reserving some lowers for others who have engaged them. Change and give me one."

"I can't do it."

"Why can't you? I tell you I couldn't sleep a wink in an upper berth. I'll give you a dollar extra if you will fix me all right."

"I am not taking bribes. All the lower berths are engaged. First come first served."

"Now see here! I am a stranger to you, but if you will give me a lower berth and some one else an upper, you won't regret it." (This was said confidentially.)

"I tell you I have no lower berth for you."

"And you won't change some one and give me a lower?"

"No."

"Then all I have to say is that you are mighty unaccommodating, and I'll report you to the Company. The idea of my climbing up into an upper berth! I tell you I couldn't sleep a wink! No, sir, not a single wink"— and the fat man walked off, very angry, and with a very red face.

VI.

CLARK returned to the hotel, had supper, and some melody from his violin, and then it was time to take the train for Columbus.

When he entered the sleeping-car, the first person he saw was the fat man, who, it seemed, had concluded to take an upper berth, after all. The fat man was removing a pair of fat boots, and the porter had placed a small step-ladder for use in ascending to the upper berth.

As Clark would be obliged to rise by two o'clock, the train being due in Columbus half an hour later, he decided to follow the fat man's example and go to bed early.

Clark's berth was directly opposite the fat man's, whose aldermanic proportions filled up all the space in that part of the car; so Clark seated himself in the drawing-room to wait until the large man should ascend into the upper berth.

The fat man, having partly prepared himself

for repose, with some display of clumsiness climbed up, and Clark heard him mumble :

" I shall not sleep a wink! No, not a single wink!"

Clark was soon in bed, and fell asleep almost instantly, and dreamed he was aboard the *Fleetwing*, off Montauk Point, surrounded by a great school of porpoises, which were puffing, blowing, and snorting in the most extraordinary manner, even for porpoises. The dream did not last long, for the dreamer soon awoke.

" No wonder I had that dream! The fat man, who could n't sleep a wink, is the cause of it. Well, when he said he could n't sleep a wink he did n't tell a lie, for no one winks when asleep. Now, if he had said he could n't sleep *quietly*, he would have hit it exactly."

Clark had never before heard such snoring as that which came from the fat man. It was an unhappy combination of puffing, blowing, and snorting, and the snort proper was so loud that the noise made by the moving train seemed profound silence in comparison. Clark soon found that he was not the only passenger who was awake and receiving the benefit of the fat man's concert, for some one called out :

"For goodness' sake, porter, do turn that elephant over occasionally, and I'll give you a dollar in the morning."

"I second the motion—of turning"—cried Clark, "and will add my subscription of a dollar."

Another voice cried :

"Ditto!"

The porter, glad of the chance for making such good fees, tried the turn-over process and found it a dangerous experiment ; for the fat man, upon being touched, awoke instantly and said in tones most emphatic :

"Just try that again, if you dare! I am away from home, and propose having my snore out! My wife is the only person who has the privilege of interfering with me in this matter. Now that you have woke me up, I shall not sleep a wink ; no, not a single wink!"

But he was soon at it again, as fiercely as ever, and no one disturbed him.

There Clark lay, wishing he might fall asleep again in spite of the fat man's snoring.

He thought :

"I wonder some one has not invented a sleeping-car with snore-proof compartments. Then, when any one went to the ticket-agent or conductor for a berth, the question could be asked: 'Do you snore?' and the traveller be located according to his reply. The trouble would be that very few persons will ever admit that they snore. Some will go so far as to say that they breathe a little hard sometimes, but I never yet met an habitual snorer who would admit that it was a regular thing with him."

As Clark lay there, wide awake, thinking of various things, his thoughts finally turned to a late bachelor friend by the name of Day, who had just married a lady much younger than himself. Now, Clark had one very bad habit—namely, that of rhyming. Not that he thought himself a poet, or that he wrote bachelor love-ditties commencing in some such familiar strain as

"Precious darling, how I love thee!
Love thee, darling, oh so much!
Search the world, my precious dearie,
I'll not find another such!"

No! Clark's verses were of an entirely different character, being rather practical than otherwise. He had sometimes found, too, that his rhyming made him sleepy. He would try the effect now. So, as he lay there thinking of Day, and wishing at the same time that the fat man would wink more and snore less, the following beautiful verses came into his poetic brain :

HAPPY DAYS.

Now, I should say that Mrs. Day
    Was not a Day past twenty ;
While Mr. D. is forty-three,
    (The difference is a plenty !)

If Mr. D. and wife agree
    And try to please each other,
The match may prove a happy move
    For one as much as t' other.

But if, alas ! it comes to pass,
    That one the other bothers,
Time will come yet they 'll both regret
    They ever left their mothers !

So let us pray that Mr. Day
    May ne'er indulge in snarling,
That Mrs. D. may always be,
    As now, his " precious darling."

> That joy and peace may never cease,
>   With Days and years increasing;
> But may each year find both more dear
>   And love prove never ceasing.
>
> But *most* we pray that neither may
>   Snore like this sleeping fat man,
> For if——

"Good-night, Day. I wish you joy. Many happy returns!"

Clark had fallen asleep, and was dreaming of Day's wedding festivities; so the rest of the poem is forever lost to the world.

How sad!

VII.

"TIME to get up for Columbus." The porter of the sleeping-car had accompanied this summons with a mild punch in Clark's side. Clark arose forthwith and dressed. At half-past two the train entered the depôt at Columbus, and Clark took a hack to the hotel. He was on the point of registering, when the clerk said:

"I am very sorry to say that we are full, every bed being occupied. We put up cots in the parlors and halls, and the last of these is taken. There is a convention here."

"How far is it to the next hotel?" asked Clark.

"Only two blocks. You might possibly find accommodations there, but it is doubtful."

Clark went to this hotel, but there was no bed for him. He was told of still another hotel not far away, and thither he went, with little hope, however. When he entered this third house, he saw at a glance that it was a very common place.

"Can I obtain a room here?" he inquired of a man in the office who had a very red nose and bloodshot eyes.

"There's one bed with two rooms in it,—hic. I mean two beds with one room in them,—hic."

"You mean one room with two beds in it, I suppose; but from what I see, I think you are *pretty full* here too," said Clark.

Another man now appeared and said:

"Here, Jim, you go to bed right away, quick! I'll show the gentleman up." Then turning to Clark, he said:

"We are overrun this week. There is one room on the top floor in which there are two beds, and only one is occupied. You can have one of the beds, if you don't object to rooming with a stranger."

"Do you know the man?"

"Yes; he is a country merchant. He's all right."

Clark decided to take what was offered him. He was tired and sleepy, and thought that any thing in the way of a bed would be preferable to sitting up the remainder of the night.

"Wait till I get a candle," said the man.

Soon they were on their way to the room. Clark followed the man through a long hall, then through a narrow passage, then up a steep flight of stairs, another passage-way, another flight of stairs, more halls, more stairs, more passage-ways, and so on and on.

It seemed a great deal like exploring a cave, for there was no light to be seen, save that of the lone, flickering candle, and the turnings were many and strange. At last the guide called out: "We are almost there," and then a draught put out the candle.

"Have you a match about you?" asked the guide.

Clark searched, but found none, so he answered:

"I have not."

"Neither have I."

"Then we are lost!" said Clark.

"Well, see here, stranger, 't is n't such a joking matter. I have been here only a few weeks, and to tell you the truth, it would puzzle me a good deal to find my way back without a light."

" What do you propose doing ? " asked Clark.

" Well, we are on the top floor, and can't be a great way from the room we want. The man in it probably has matches. Now, let me think a minute. Here's the top of the stairs. Now by going on to the end of this hall, then to the left, and a short turn to the right, I think we shall fetch it. If we don't hit it the first time, we'll come mighty close to it. Oh, we'll find it."

" Go on, my brave man. I'll follow thee," said Clark.

They went feeling their way along for a while, and then the guide said :

"I don't think we are on the right track after all. I'm sort of turned around."

" I should think you would have light-houses here and there. If we can't find the room, I suppose we must drop anchor and ' lay to ' till daylight."

They had proceeded into the cave a little farther when the guide stopped, gave a stamp, and exclaimed : " What a fool I am ! "

"What's the matter now?" asked Clark.

"Nothing—only I had forgotten about this man. No trouble to find him! Just listen!"

"I hear a noise like unto the united efforts of a number of swine," said Clark.

"That's *him!*"

"It never rains but it pours—that is, he never breathes but he snores," muttered Clark.

"Do you object to rooming with a man who snores?" queried the guide.

"Have you a lounge anywhere upon which I can lie down?" asked Clark, instead of answering the guide's question.

"Yes, down-stairs in the parlor there's one. But we must get some matches. You don't want to take that bed, then?"

"No, I thank you. I had a taste of this kind of thing on a sleeping-car to-night."

"You don't mean to tell me you ever heard any one snore like this before?"

"No; not just in this style. This is more suggestive of *stile*, more à la swine than anything I ever heard before," said Clark.

"I suppose he will think it is a trifle strange to be woke up for matches at this time of night," said the guide.

"I should think it likely! Do you know the man well?"

"Yes, he used to board at the Sun Hotel in Dodgeville when I was clerking there. I have met him only once since I came here."

"Well, knock away!"

The guide rapped gently.

No answer, but the man snored on.

The guide knocked harder, and again still harder, and soon there was a change in the style of the person within, the grunts becoming less regular, and at last he awoke.

"Who's there?"

"Me; Jack Hart."

"I don't know you."

"Yes, you do. I used to work at the 'Sun.'"

("I'll warrant he wishes you were at the sun now," whispered Clark.)

"Well, what do you want, anyhow?"

"I want some matches."

"Matches! What do you mean by bothering me for matches at this time of the night! I don't believe you are Jack Hart. What is my name?"

"Smith."

("That was n't a hard conundrum; any one could have guessed that," said Clark, softly.)

"Who is that other fellow with you?"

"A traveller from the East."

("You should have said a wise man from the East," again whispered Clark.)

"What 's he doing along with you, anyhow?"

"That is a tough question and it will take a world of explanation," whispered Clark.

"That 's a fact!" said the guide.

"If you tell him just how and why I happen to be here, and that I don't like his style of snoring it may make him mad, and then he will not give us any matches. Tell him you were showing me to a room and the candle went out."

The guide so stated.

"What does all this whispering mean, I 'd like to know. I believe you are a couple of sneak thieves or worse. I 'll poke some matches through the keyhole, and then you fellows just git!"

When the guide had received the matches and lighted the candle he again led the way, and in the course of time they were out of the cave.

Clark lay down on a lounge in the parlor and was soon fast asleep, not awakening till eight o'clock.

He made a hasty toilet in the " wash-room," paid his bill, and then went to the hotel where he had first applied for accommodations.

There had been a number of departures by the morning trains, and Clark was given a large and handsomely furnished room. He had an excellent breakfast, and this, together with his pleasant room and a short intercourse with his precious violin, soon put him in good spirits.

VIII.

CLARK'S business experiences in Columbus are not worthy of special notice. He did very little there, and was glad when the time came to move on to Cincinnati.

The train for Cincinnati arrived at Columbus from the East one hour late, and continued to lose time after leaving Columbus. It was one A.M. when Clark reached his destination. He had telegraphed for a room, and was given very pleasant quarters.

"Now, I'll have my sleep out this time. I haven't averaged six hours out of the twenty-four so far on this trip, and I feel used up," thought Clark, as he put out the gas and opened the window before getting into bed. He slept soundly until about five o'clock, when he awoke, and with one bound sprang out of bed with the exclamation: "The house is on fire!" The next moment he had grasped his violin, expecting to have to run for its life and his own. The room was filled with smoke almost to suffocation, but Clark now discovered that the source of all the trouble was a large chimney across the street, out of which was pouring dense volumes of soft-coal smoke. It was a rainy day, and this smoke seemed to make a bee-line for Clark's open window. He also discovered that his spasmodic cry of "The house is on fire!" was making trouble, for the occupant of an adjoining room—a woman—was now screaming: "Fire! fire!" at the top of her voice.

In a twinkling there was great commotion in the house; many took up the cry of "Fire! fire!" and the screaming and general confusion was something which Clark will never forget.

He had closed his window, and now, in his bare feet, and with a linen duster thrown over his night-gown, was in the hall, where he beheld men, women, and children, many of them in more scant attire than himself, rushing about. Some were carrying their clothes, and all were bent upon leaving the rapidly burning building as hastily as their legs would permit.

"The fire is out! No danger! It's all right!" cried Clark, as he ran through the halls, "up stairs and down stairs, and in other persons' chambers," trying to quiet the panic-stricken guests. He succeeded pretty well, and by the time the steam fire-engines came flying up to the hotel comparative quiet reigned again.

"After all this row of my own manufacture I don't believe I shall have my sleep out, after all," thought Clark. He found he was too wide-awake to sleep any more, and so dressed and went down stairs. It was too early for breakfast, and he took a walk across the bridge, to Covington, Ky., and return. When he went in to breakfast, every one was talking about the fire. The fact that there had really been no fire was not yet known to the guests, and poor Clark was obliged to hear conversation like the following:

"How fortunate it was that the fire was put out before it made much headway."

"Yes. In what part of the house was the fire anyhow?"

" I don't know."

",If it had n't been for that lady, who first discovered it, giving the alarm so promptly, we might have all been burned up."

" That 's a fact. But that tall man in a long duster showed great presence of mind, and quieted the frantic ones before the fire was really out."

" So I understand. Do you know his name ? "

" No, I don't. He ought to have a vote of thanks from the guests. We must lead in the matter, and find out who he is."

Thus did the conversation run on, and Clark felt more sheepish every moment. He would not have been surprised had the wool come out all over him. In fact he did actually say, " Bah !" and left the table without eating much breakfast. As he entered the hotel office a bell-boy handed him a note. It was a request from the proprietor to call at the private office.

Clark called forthwith. Of course it was about the fire. The occupant of the room adjoining Clark's was a sister of the proprietor,

and she had told her brother about Clark's cry
of "The house is on fire!" The proprietor
wanted to know what it all meant. Clark explained. The host, who was of goodly proportions, leaned back in his chair and laughed
until Clark feared one person would yet be
seriously injured by the fire. When the proprietor had subsided, he said to Clark:

"Don't be distressed over this matter. Your
fire has done no damage. On the contrary, it
has been a good thing; for the fire-hose with
which this house is supplied has, through your
agency, been found to be unfit for use. The
very servants, too, whose duty it is to turn firemen on such an occasion, rushed to their rooms
to save their personal effects, and some of them
left the hotel on a run and have not yet returned. I suppose they are running yet!"

Clark went to his room, and, taking up his
violin, played "Scotland's Burning"; after
which he ran into something more classic,
and then, samples in hand, he went forth to
solicit orders.

IX.

CLARK again went through the experience of finding himself one among many salesmen, all bent upon presenting the merits of their respective wares, in the most favorable light possible, to the various buyers.

During the morning he met no less than nine salesmen representing firms competing with his own, and while he was familiar with the saying, "Competition is the *life* of trade," he could not help feeling that it would have been more agreeable to have had less "life" and fewer competitors in town that day.

He mused: "I thought I knew what competition was, but a few days' experience as a commercial traveller has taught me that we who remain at home know very little of how our travellers have to work and scheme for trade."

Clark did nothing that morning further than to have short conversations with several buyers, two of whom appointed certain hours in the afternoon for looking at samples of keels and hearing prices.

With one exception all the buyers were very courteous and sociable. Their offices were thrown wide open to the visiting salesmen, all who called were invited to be seated, and every thing was conducted in a pleasant manner. In one office Clark was told: "I'm sorry to be obliged to put you off till Monday, but we will be glad to figure with you then, at eleven in the morning, if that hour will suit you. If you have any writing to do there is a desk here at your disposal."

Another buyer said: "There are several salesmen ahead of you, Mr. Clark, but I shall have finished with them this morning. If you will call at two o'clock I shall be ready for you. Or, come to lunch with me at one o'clock and after that we can transact our business."

Clark accepted the invitation, and the lunch proved to be a most palatable repast. After this, buyer and seller returned to the store and Clark took a good order, without a hitch. Everywhere there was a genuine hospitality shown Clark in Cincinnati, with one exception.

This "Exception" to the heartiness and agreeableness of Cincinnati's buyers was a man who, instead of having an office where commercial travellers could be comfortably seated while transacting business, had a little place fenced in, kept sacred for his own use, the salesman standing on the outside of the sanctum. It was a wire office, and the man inside had a somewhat savage countenance. Altogether there was considerable of a caged-animal air about the wire enclosure.

To be sure, there was a place in another part of the store, where travellers were sometimes invited to display their samples, when numerous, the caged animal then coming out to devour them—the samples, not the travellers.

Clark called on this person at about four o'clock. The man was in his cage, writing.

Clark waited a few moments before introducing himself, and as he looked at the man he thought of lines in a Primer, as follows:

"This is a Bear. He is in his Cage. If you put your Hand in the Cage He will Bite you!"

Clark presented his card. The man looked

at it, said "In a minute," and kept on writing. Clark waited uneasily for fully five minutes, and then said:

"Can you give me a few moments' attention? If not, I'll go."

The man in the cage looked up, and said in a patronizing tone:

"Well, sir, what can I do for you?"

Now, Clark interpreted this "Well, sir, what can I do for you?" thus:

"Well, sir, what do you want? You are here in distress, and have come to ask a favor. I'm weary of beggars!" so Clark said:

"Oh, I'm not in any trouble. I'm neither hungry, thirsty, nor sick, and I'm pretty well off for clothes."

The man in the cage appeared somewhat startled at this reply, and looked sharply at Clark.

Then he said:

"I suppose you are here to sell goods. If you have any specially low prices to quote, let's have them."

Clark gave quotations on hulls and other goods, and the man in the cage said:

"I think you have something back of these prices, something lower."

The man had gaped continually while hearing Clark's figures, so when the man questioned the prices, Clark could not resist saying :

"A man with as *open a countenance* as you have should not be suspicious."

The man in the cage looked sharply at Clark again but probably did not see the drift of the remark.

"I have my samples of keels with me," said Clark.

"Don't care to look at them. Am full. But if you will give me five per cent. off of the price you quoted on hulls, I'll buy some."

"I don't want your order at any different price than that which I named," said Clark.

The man then said that Clark could send such and such a quantity of several articles, but he fought for lower prices on every thing. During all this transaction the man in the cage had occupied a large arm-chair, Clark having to stand outside meanwhile—very *mean* while, he thought.

This was Clark's first and last experience on

his trip of being treated, as he thought, rudely. The other buyers of Cincinnati had been so very hospitable and pleasant that the actions of the man in the cage stood out all the more glaringly.

One buyer had named five o'clock that afternoon for Clark to call.

This person would have been able to have given Clark his undivided attention, had it not been for the telephone. Clark was interrupted by calls from that little bell four or five times within half an hour, and he wished the telephone had never been invented. It was certainly far from pleasant when, as the buyer was apparently ready to begin giving an order, some one should wring the order from Clark's grasp, so to speak, by simply ringing that little bell. Then, too, the conversation at the telephone was necessarily uninteresting to Clark, by reason of its one-sidedness—as for example:

Ding-a-ling-a-ling!

"Well, who is it?"

"Can't understand you."

"Talk louder."

"Now I get you."

"Well."
"What's that?"
"Oh!"
"Yes."
"When?"
"I'll try."
"No."
"Well."
"Can't say."
"Perhaps."
"Will if I can."
"Not at all."
"Is that really a fact?"
"Ha! ha! ha!"
"Can't."
"Good-bye."

Clark did no business with this person, and he firmly believed that the telephone was the cause of his failure.

One buyer whom he met that day had numerous large photographs of commercial travellers hanging on the walls of his office. He called this his "Art Gallery," forgetting, perhaps, that the commercial traveller is the most artless of mortals!

In the evening, Clark was one of a party of eight commercial travellers who took supper together at the hotel.

Clark had made the acquaintance of his fellow "tourists" at Pittsburgh and Cincinnati.

They all went in company to the theatre that evening, to see a celebrated English actor.

X.

"I AM thankful to-morrow will be Sunday. No talking to be done for a while over quality of goods and prices. I'll go to Louisville by steamer Monday night, and so shall have no long car rides until I leave Louisville for Indianapolis. Commercial travelling is the hardest business I ever got into. What with travelling at night to make time and working all day to make sales, there isn't much time for any rest."

Clark was ruminating; but he did not spend much time in this way. He was tired and sleepy, having had three successive poor nights. After a little music from his violin he went to bed and was soon asleep, his last thoughts being that he was glad he should not have to hear anything about business, goods, or prices on the morrow.

When he awoke the following morning he found that he had been mistaken in thinking he should have a quiet Sunday, free from all hints of business, for two commercial travellers, of the Jewish persuasion, and both of them in the clothing line, occupied the rooms on each side of him. They had already commenced receiving customers and were setting forth the merits of their wares most eloquently. From the loud tones of one of these salesmen, Clark judged there was a deaf customer to be dealt with. Now, Clark could have no reasonable grudge against these people for doing business on Sunday. It was not *their* Sabbath. Still, before he had heard them in operation long, he went down to the office and asked to have his room changed.

The clerk seemed surprised, and said:

"We cannot give you as pleasant a room anywhere else. What objection have you to your present quarters?"

"The room is very pleasant; but I want to spend a quiet Sunday."

"Is it particularly noisy where you are?"

"It might be worse. But can't you give me a room not next door to any salesmen who should keep Saturday instead of Sunday. Understand, I am not finding fault with my neighbors, who are Jews, for working to-day. Not at all—but I would prefer to be where I can read and write in peace to-day."

The clerk gave Clark another room which, though two flights higher up, was pleasant enough.

It was a beautiful day, and soon after nine o'clock Clark started off for a long walk, with the intention of attending church wherever he might find himself at the proper hour. He crossed the Ohio over a fine bridge, and within half an hour was fairly in the country. It was a very pretty country, too, with its quaint Kentucky homes, and fields of waving corn. Soon a village, or perhaps it was a city, came in view. There was no scarcity of churches, and the bells were ringing for the last time. Clark being an Episcopalian made inquiries of a person he met, and was directed to the church of that denomination.

When he entered this church the organist was playing the voluntary and Clark recognized the piece as being a selection from that very churchly composition, namely: the Opera of Faust! "Alas," thought Clark, "have I indeed run afoul of one of those churches where the organist and choir try to *spread* themselves? It looks very much like it. There's the quartette, with their sheets of music, looking very important!"

The voluntary being ended what a change, what a contrast to this secular music, when the minister pronounced in solemn tones: "The Lord is in his Holy Temple; let all the earth keep silence before him," Faust still ringing in the ears of the congregation!

The music for the *Venite* executed—more properly *murdered*—by the choir that morning was a very intricate composition. Sung by a good quartette, it is a treat to any lover of good music to listen to it.

Clark was familiar with the music, and although he had never been considered a nervous man, he felt very much on edge when they launched out on this *Venite;* for, from the start, it was plain there were no singers in that choir. Were the congregation not familiar with the service they could not have told in what language the choir were trying to sing, the words were mumbled and jumbled together in so fantastic a fashion.

There was not the slightest difficulty in telling who was the leader of the choir, for the basso was always perceptibly ahead! There were some bad breaks, but at last in a hop-skip-and-jump style, the choir finished the *Venite*, and the congregation gave a great sigh of relief. Even the minister looked easier. There was whispering now going on in the choir, and Clark turned his head in that direction a moment. He concluded the situation was about as follows: The organist was affirming solemnly that he was all right. The basso was hinting the tenor was at fault. The tenor knows he was O K but is certain the basso was n't. The soprano and contralto were too much put out with each other, and with everybody else, to venture saying any thing, but their looks spoke volumes.

The music for the *Te Deum*, the next important piece on the programme, was also a difficult composition, with many twists and pitfalls. There is one portion of it which sounds very much like an old-fashioned school "round." In the part referred to, one singer starts up, then another, and another, and so on until each member of the quartette is doing his or her best to keep in the crooked path laid out. Clark was again on edge, for he knew of the traps set in this piece to ensnare.

"I wonder how the soprano will manage those high notes in her solo," he thought. "She is getting into dangerous waters. The waves grow higher farther out at sea. Wait till she strikes the high C." It was a squeal, but she did it.

Now they were coming to the "round," and entered boldly; but, lo! while in the middle of this part the organ sighed, groaned, gave one unearthly scream, and then refused to respond to the touch of the organist. The blowers—two boys who had shown themselves between the pieces—had let the wind out. Perhaps they had quarrelled, and ceased blowing in order that they might have free use of their arms and fists for blows of a different kind.

Both basso and tenor rushed behind the organ, but the boys were pumping again with all their might.

The *Te Deum* went on minus the "round," but no further intricate music was attempted that day, and Clark was surprised to find that the choir could stoop so low as to sing some good old chants and hymns.

Clark sang, and others near him joined in

with their voices until the choir were pretty effectually drowned. Indeed, the whole congregation gradually warmed up and sang—a state of things which Clark believed was not often permitted in that church.

Had the choir not broken down in the *Te Deum*, it is not at all likely that they would have condescended to sing any thing in which the "common people" could join.

After the sermon, Clark began his return tramp to Cincinnati. For a short distance he was entertained by a discussion over the music, carried on by two men who were walking just ahead of him.

"There's no use in our standing this attempt at operatic music any longer, and I for one mean to put my foot down on it at once."

"It is disagreeable, but I fear 't will make a row in the parish if we stir the matter up."

"Well, let it. I wish to goodness we had never got the new organ; then our organist would never have tried to give us the opera, nor the singers attempted to ape expert city choirs."

Clark heard no more of this conversation, for the men had turned off into a side street.

XI.

HIS first call, Monday morning, was upon a firm doing business in a handsome five-story building near the hotel. He was told by one of the clerks that the buyer was to be found in the rear office. As Clark entered this office he saw, seated at a desk, a person whom he supposed to be the buyer, and so presented the card of Dale & Clark, saying as usual: "My name is Clark."

The individual addressed did not even look up, but kept his head down, at the same time having one hand raised as if to shield his eyes from the light.

Clark imagined the man was deaf, so he raised his voice: "My name is Clark, of the firm of Dale & Clark."

The man placed a hand to one ear—still shielding his eyes with the other hand—and said: "A little louder, please."

Clark braced himself, took a long breath, and

in such a tone as he might have employed in hailing a distant vessel, cried out : " My name is Clark, of the firm of Dale & Clark."

" Beg your pardon, but did you say your name was Stark ? "

" No ; *Clark*—C-l-a-r-k."

" Oh, *Lark*. Well, go on."

The man still kept his hand in front of his eyes, and Clark felt very much embarrassed.

" I am making a business trip for our firm," howled Clark.

" Making a trip for fun, did you say ? " asked the man.

Clark gave himself an extra brace and yelled : " No ! I-am-making-a-trip-for-our-firm."

" *Whose* firm ? "

" Dale & Clark."

" Oh, now I understand you. Beg your pardon. A competitor of yours is here to-day, and we are intending to give him a large order for every thing which we need in your line—so there is no chance for you ! "

This was a strange speech, and Clark was much taken aback. The deaf man continued : " The truth of the matter is, we need lots of goods, car-loads, in fact. If you had come a few days earlier, and offered to sell to us at seventy-five per cent. less than any one else would, we *might* have bought a train-load of you."

Clark was puzzled still more, and began to think the man was drunk.

" We will look into matters, however, in the course of a week or two," continued the man, " and in the meantime please call in to see us twice a day."

This *was* strange. Clark could not seem to find words for utterance, but stood almost as motionless as a statue. The man still held his hand over his eyes, so that Clark could see very little of his face, and after a short pause, said : " Have a seat, Mr. Lark. You'll find a Cincinnati paper here not over a month old. In the course of a few hours I'll talk to you. Don't be in a hurry."

Clark now looked about him for the first time, and saw that the book-keeper and several other persons in the office were shaking with laughter.

The deaf man looked up and held out his hand to Clark, saying : " Old messmate, how are you ? "

He was not the buyer at all, nor was his hearing bad. He was a jocular friend with whom Clark had made a cruise the summer before in the *Fleetwing*, and had come to Cincinnati to attend a wedding. He was to leave for New York that afternoon. Clark was now introduced to the real buyer—a cousin of Clark's friend,—who proved to be a very agreeable man. He gave Clark a good order, and invited him to dinner. It was a good dinner, too, and Clark enjoyed it.

CHAPTER XII.

CLARK had finished his business in Cincinnati, and was aboard the Louisville steamer.

This boat had a large number of passengers aboard. Clark went to the clerk's office, and was given a key to a state-room. Upon opening the door he was surprised to find another person's luggage in the room. Returning at once to the office, he said to the clerk:

"You have made a mistake, giving me a room which is already occupied."

"No mistake about it at all. We can't give a passenger a room to himself when the boat is as full as it is to-day. If we did, half the passengers would sit up. There are two berths in each room."

"I supposed I paid for my room and was entitled to it."

"No, sir. There is no extra charge for rooms or meals. You paid your fare, which entitles you to a berth, but not to a whole room."

"I thought you ran these boats the same as is done on the Sound, and other Eastern routes,—that is, charged so much for passage, and an additional dollar or more for a room. I don't want to room with a stranger, and would rather pay double fare, and will do so if you give me a room to myself."

"Every thing is taken except one room in a pretty warm part of the boat. You can have that."

"I'll take it," said Clark. "How much more shall I pay you?"

"Nothing extra."

When he entered this room it was pretty warm. The floor was almost hot to the touch, the boilers being directly underneath.

He was disappointed to find no wash-bowl nor water in the room.

He again went to the clerk, and reported there were no conveniences for washing, and requested that basin, water, and towels be supplied.

"We don't furnish such things in the rooms,"

said the clerk. "You will find a wash-room in connection with the bar and barber-shop."

Clark found his way to the wash-room. Long towels, already much soiled, hung on rollers, and he saw at once that his best plan was to make the acquaintance of the barber. Clark went to his state-room and got out his soap, brush, and razor, and was soon on the best terms with the barber, who, while shaving Clark, gave an account of his experiences during the "wah."

He had been a slave in Alabama, but ran away the first year of the conflict, arriving North safely. But although he found himself his own master, liberty proved to have many hardships, and he was so homesick to see his wife and children, that he made several attempts to return to "de ole plantation."

Finally he was "gobbled up by de Union pickets." An army officer took a fancy to him, and made him body-servant. He remained with this officer till the close of the war, and then went in search of his family, finding them safe and sound on the old plantation; but "ole massa" had been killed in one of the last battles, and the estate had changed hands. "With massa gone dead, an' de kind missus and all de kind children gone away, I 'se mos' heart-broken, and we could n't stay thar no mo'; so we came to Louisville, an' we are doin' right smart, sah!" concluded the barber.

During Clark's stay in the barber-shop, the steamer had been going down the river rapidly, and when he went out on deck the high, green banks of the "Old Kentucky Shore" stood forth in all their beauty. It reminded him of the beautiful Connecticut up which he had sailed in the *Fleetwing*. Many pretty houses, with broad verandas, dotted the Kentucky side of the river, and there was nothing wanting to make it a perfect river scene, save the presence of sailing craft. Not a sail did Clark see. Probably the swiftness of the current and the numerous shoals prevent yachting to any extent on the Ohio. Clark now began to feel hungry. On going into the main saloon, he saw supper was already in progress. He took a seat between two gentlemen, and as he did so he noticed that some of those at the table looked at him rather sharply for a moment. Clark was astonished to find such a sumptuous repast as the one now spread before him. He was hungry, and enjoyed the good things very much. It was a very lively company, too, and Clark thought that, for a chance collection of travellers, they seemed very well acquainted with each other. The conversation was spirited and often witty. When wine of various kinds, including champagne, began to flow freely around that table, Clark was more astonished than before.

"Why, this is a long way ahead of ocean travel!" he thought.

The wine having been discussed, certain persons were called upon for speeches.

"I wonder no writer has ever given us an account of how they do things on Ohio River steamers," thought Clark. "Here, for the small sum of three dollars, you can travel miles and miles,—no charge for state-rooms, and an opportunity given for every passenger to get drunk on the best of wines! I don't see how there can be a cent in it, the way some of these men drink!"

But the first speech was now being made, and a crowd had gathered around the table.

The captain and others connected with the Louisville Packet Line were thanked, "in the name of the Common Council of Cincinnati, for the pleasant excursion and bountiful repast,"— and then Clark longed to find a hole into which he might drop out of sight, for he had unwittingly seated himself at a table to which only a favored few had been invited! The regular supper for the passengers had not yet commenced. At first he thought he ought to arise and explain, but decided it would be the wiser plan to keep quiet and sit it out. He was relieved when the last speech had been made and the party arose and dispersed.

Clark again went forward and enjoyed the scenery very much. Gradually there were less and less of habitations, and at a point where no dwelling was to be seen the steamer took aboard four passengers. The party consisted of a very old man and woman, and a younger couple verging on fifty. It soon became whispered around that these were two newly married couples, starting out on their wedding journey to Louisville. Clark could credit this report so far as it related to the younger couple,—

though he thought they were old enough to know better,—but the other pair appeared any thing but bridal. All four found seats near Clark, and fell in with an acquaintance to whom the old man told the whole story of their courtship, speaking in tones which could be heard by all on the forward deck. The old man said: "You see, we—thet is me and the old woman—hed no idee of sich a thing as gettin' spliced till one day Jeemes let on thet he was sorter smit with Maria. Maria, you know, is the name of her gal, and Jeemes is my boy. Wal, Maria, by the way, is forty-seving or tharabouts,—can't tell 'zackly, 'cause she 's a woman,—haw! haw! haw!—and Jeemes he's forty-nine come November. Wal, my wife thet now is did n't take to partin' with her gal, no how, and I did n't like to let my boy go. Could n't spare him now thet I own no nigger. The United States oughter pay me for thet nigger. Wal, sez I to Mrs. Jorkins thet then was, but now is Mrs. Rangley—haw! haw! haw!—sez I: 'Mrs. Jorkins' (her old man 's been gone these thirty years), sez I: 'Mrs. Jorkins, thar 's just one way of a-fixin' this 'ere bizness, and thet is for you to hitch on to me. My house is big enough fer all on us, an' I hev a right smart lot of pigs and things, and forty acres in corn to fatten 'em on. Let 's all git spliced to onct, and live at my house like the Happy Family we 've hearn of at Barnum's!' 'Thet ain't no bad idee,' sez Mrs. Jorkins thet then was, but now is Mrs. Rangley—haw! haw! haw!—' an' I 'll feel Maria on the subjec', an' if she sez do it, why it don't make no 'ticular difference to me, and I 'll be thar!' Well, Maria, it seems, sez, 'Take him up!' and she tuck me up; and here we all is, right from the 'squire's; and I think it 's a good 'rangement—don't you?" There was a chorus of yeses and not a little merriment when the old man closed his story.

When Clark got into his narrow bed he found it very warm and very hard. If he opened the door which communicated with the deck it would let in the cool air, but there would be nothing to prevent a thief from coming in and robbing him. "I 'll leave the door open a while, but will not go to sleep without closing and locking it," thought Clark. But he *did* fall asleep, though it was an accident, and when he awoke the next morning his door was as he had left it, wide open, and the steamer was lying quietly at the Louisville levee.

Clark had put his waistcoat, in a pocket of which were his watch and money, under the mattress. This was safe, but he looked in vain for his pantaloons.

Nothing else was missing, but he would almost have preferred to have had his watch taken just then than those trousers. He called one of the colored waiters, who came and listened to Clark's tale. The colored boy reported the loss to the clerk, and that official came and condoled with Clark, reminding him at the same time that to leave an outside door open on a steamer containing all kinds of people was a very risky thing to do.

"As I have no other suit with me my best plan will be to send some one up-town to purchase a pair of pantaloons," said Clark.

"I can lend you a pair, if you will accept them. Then you can make your own selection at some store," said the clerk.

Clark took in the size of the clerk, and concluded there would be some trouble getting into the pantaloons, but nevertheless said: "Thank you; I will accept yours gladly. But perhaps mine may be somewhere on deck or elsewhere on board. The thief most likely wanted them for the contents of the pockets and may have thrown them in some corner."

"I'll have a thorough search made," said the clerk. "Was there much in the pockets?"

"Very little. A knife, some loose change, and—goodness!—the keys to my trunk and valise."

"That's unfortunate," said the clerk.

"For the thief?"

"Well, I was thinking of your keys—but 't was a poor haul for the thief! I'll have that search made at once."

Nothing was found of the stolen articles. The clerk's pantaloons proved to be of very limited dimensions for Clark. They were several inches too short, and several degrees too tight.

"Are they a success?" asked the clerk, opening the door a little.

"A *limited* success," said Clark; "but I am thankful for them all the same."

Clark entered a hack, and was driven to a clothing store, where he tried on and on, but did not find a fit. Finally the clothier said he could make Clark a pair in the course of the day.

"What am I to do in the meantime?" asked Clark.

"Oh, I 'll lend you the nearest fitting of these until to-morrow morning."

Clark selected the goods, was measured, and then, arrayed in another pair of borrowed pantaloons, went to the hotel and had breakfast. After this, he hunted up a locksmith. It took over an hour to fit keys to valise and trunk, but when this was at last accomplished Clark gave a little time to his violin, and was then ready for business.

XIII.

ALL the Louisville merchants whom Clark met that day were Southern men, save one. This exception was a man by the name of Vogel, who was by birth a Pennsylvania Dutchman. Vogel had lived in Louisville for the past fifteen years, but he still spoke English in a manner peculiar to his tribe.

Vogel was the buying partner of a prosperous Louisville firm. It was toward the close of the day when Clark called upon him. The Dutchman chanced to speak of his old home in Pennsylvania. Clark, who had several times gone trouting in the county in which Vogel formerly lived, had considerable to relate which was interesting to the Dutchman—who with great fervor exclaimed again and again.

"Vell! vell! Ish dot so!"

Nothing short of Clark's going to supper and spending the night at Vogel's home would suffice.

Vogel lived a distance of nearly six miles in the country. It was a splendid drive, and a smart span of horses, owned by Vogel, soon carried them to the Dutchman's home. As they drove up to the house Clark noticed the great number of cabbages growing in the garden; enough to supply the whole city of Louisville, he thought.

"Dot ish mine gabbage orchart," said Vogel, who then explained that he had a large family.

It was a rather peculiar supper to which Clark sat down that evening.

The substantials consisted of fried fresh pork, boiled cabbage, sauer-kraut, and Limburger cheese—very old.

Not one of these things was exactly a favorite dish with Clark, but he was very hungry, and ate heartily, trusting that his usual good digestion would hold out.

It did not, however, for he went to bed feeling very much as though he had been dining on lead.

Being tired he soon fell into an uneasy sleep and had strange visions, culminating in a singular dream which we venture recording here.

He was a boy again—a bad boy, too, having run away from school to go a-fishing. He was in the woods and had a pole and line but no hooks, having by accident swallowed the latter, which were giving him much pain.

He sat down by a little waterfall, beneath which he was sure trout were lying in wait. The bad boy was wondering how, having "played hooky," he could come into possession of the articles which were necessary to enable him to do some *real* hooking.

Suddenly a wagon stopped close to him and the bad boy heard the driver say: "Vell! vell! Ish dot so!"—and the bad boy recognized the face and voice of Vogel.

Being told to jump into the wagon the bad boy did so, and sat down upon an enormous Limburger cheese.

The wagon was loaded with these great cheeses and barrels of sauer-kraut.

In his vision the bad boy saw pails of sauer-kraut and Limburger cheeses growing as flowers by the wayside; and some lines came into his head, running as follows:—

"By roadside way, yea all about,
Blooms that fair flower, the Sauer-kraut;
Limburger, too, sweet as a rose,
Greets everywhere the upturned nose!"

Two great temples now loomed up. One was, in form and general appearance, like unto a cabbage, while the other was of Limburger style of architecture.

The wagon stopped before the first temple, and two priests came out to meet it. Their robes were made of cabbage-leaves; and, as they stood before the wagon swinging censers, in which were burning cabbages, they muttered something which, to the bad boy, seemed to be a combination of Greek, Latin, and Pennsylvania Dutch. At last the bad boy heard plainly the magic word "Sauer-kraut!" whereupon the barrels containing that article dropped out of the wagon, one by one, formed a true military line, and marched into the temple. The B. B. could see them standing there, "rank and file" (especially the *former*). "Even a cabbage-head may be taught something, if properly manipulated," thought the B. B.

The wagon now moved on to the other temple, and was met by two priests after the Order of Limburger. These latter priests were very yellow both in costumes and countenances, and this sallow look made them appear very bilious and unhappy. The B. B. wondered whether they might not be a kind of walking cheeses themselves; and, from the distress their expression and color betokened, he thought they must have a gnawing at the heart—of mice. There was more gibberish gone through with, but at the magic word "Limburger!" the cheeses commenced dancing about at a fearful rate, and the B. B. felt himself being carried around by the one on which he had been sitting. While going through a peculiar figure, which the B. B. believed to be a kind of German (Pennsylvania), his cheese gave a high jump and pitched him out of the wagon!

Clark awoke forthwith, and found he had fallen out of bed and was flat on the floor. It was broad daylight, and, looking out of his window, he saw Vogel in the garden gazing lovingly upon the growing cabbages.

XIV.

CLARK'S new pantaloons proved to be entirely satisfactory, and he again walked forth, comfortable in mind and body.

His visit in Louisville was not a business success. Vogel gave him a fair order, but further than this Clark did nothing. There were so many travellers in the city representing competing houses, that Clark seemed to have no chance. Probably he did not push himself forward as much as he should have done. Then, too, it seemed to him that being personally acquainted helped a salesman greatly with Southern buyers—not that they would pay an acquaintance or friend any more for goods than they would a stranger, but, all else being *equal*, the salesman whom they knew personally would have the preference—but that is the case to a greater or less extent everywhere. Whatever the cause, Clark took his departure from Louisville with only one order.

At a station about midway between Louisville and Indianapolis, a regular swarm of children and babies came aboard the train.

Clark thought their ages might range from four or five weeks old to three or four years.

"There has been a baby-show," thought Clark. The whole company of little ones were in charge of one man, a woman, and a girl. The man had taken the seat next in front of the one occupied by Clark, and Clark found himself counting the little ones. There were two children in the seat with the man, besides the two babies held in his arms, which number was at that moment further augmented by the woman placing another baby in his lap, saying : "Here, John, you must take care of this other trip."

"That makes five in charge of the man," thought Clark. "Two tiny ones with the woman is seven; those two fighting for a seat at the window is nine; two little ones with the girl is eleven. There are three others distributed around, crying because they can't be with 'pop' or 'mum,' as they call them—making fourteen, and throwing in the girl there are fifteen; but of course it can't be all one family, for they are too near of an age."

While Clark was still wondering and conjecturing, the woman cried out :

"John, be careful of the trips, and don't fall asleep and drop them!"

"I'll be careful, wife. Don't fret yourself," and John gave the triplets a triple squeeze, and laughed good-naturedly.

"Look out for the first twins. Victoria will catch cold if she falls asleep with the window open. Better shut it, John."

Clark offered to close the window, and this done the man asked :

"Are you acquainted in Ohio?"

"I was never west of Buffalo until this month," replied Clark.

"We are moving to Ohio from Indiana. I have a brother in Ohio, a farmer like myself. Have bought the farm adjoining his. We are a pretty big family, as you can see, to travel about much, but we could n't spare one of them. Not one too many, are there, trips?"

"Are they all here?" asked Clark.

"Every one of them. Two sets of twins, two of trips, and the rest are scattering."

This information was imparted with evident

pride, and the wife nodded approvingly. "Thirteen is a good many!" said the man, after a short pause; "but they will all be taken care of."

"*Fifteen*, you mean, John!" said the wife, reproachfully.

"*To* be sure! I'm always forgetting to reckon in the last twins. Indiana is a good farming State, and I hated to break up there, but I shall be glad to live near my brother; he and I are twins. Indiana is all right, and I don't go back on it. I tell you they raise as large crops down there as anywhere in the world."

"I should never question that for an instant," said Clark, as he looked around on the family before him. John seemed very warm with three little babies in his lap and a child on each side of him. Suddenly he turned to Clark, and said:

"If you will be so good as to hold two of these trips while I take off my coat and go get a glass of water, I'll be much obliged to you. It's hot here!"

Clark's experience in baby-holding was very

limited. The last time he held one it seemed to him as though it was going to drop to pieces, it was so limber. What, then, could he do with two?

"They won't cry, sir; they'll be good"; and before Clark could find words to protest, two triplets were handed to him, John retaining the third.

"Bless me, John, he does n't know any thing about babies. He don't even know how to hold them!" cried the alarmed mother, as she saw Clark's clumsy endeavors to handle the little ones. Poor Clark was warmer than John had even been. He was relieved beyond what pen or tongue can express when the experienced father took the two trips.

"You are not used to babies?" queried John.

"No, sir; not at all."

"None of your own, perhaps?"

"None."

"Well, well, that's a pity! Wife not living?"

"I was never married."

"Oh! *that's* it."

Clark saw numerous smiles. The whole car

was smiling, in fact; so he changed the subject, asking: "Shall I get you a glass of water?"

"Yes; I'll be much obliged to you. We are all pretty well occupied, you see."

"Yes; I see you are."

Clark went for the water, and as he was returning with some he said to John:

"Perhaps your wife would like a drink too."

"Thank you; I would," said the woman. She drank all the glass would hold, and then Clark went back and brought some for the man. After this all the children, who by word or sign could make their wants known, asked for a drink, and Clark saw he was again furnishing amusement for the other passengers as he went back and forth in his new occupation of water-carrier. At last he had gone the rounds and relieved the thirst of all the twins, triplets, and scatterings.

The train arrived at Indianapolis about midnight. Clark was feeling pretty tired, for his rest had been broken continually since his departure from New York. He was a strong advocate for every one having at least eight hours' sleep out of the twenty-four, but had come to the conclusion that all good rules relating to eating and sleeping could not be followed by a commercial traveller.

He had undressed and was just going to put the gas out when a baby in the next room commenced crying most vigorously. It was a young baby's voice, but possessed of great power. Soon there was tramping up and down the room, and Clark could hear a man's voice singing to the baby. The words of the song could not be understood by Clark, and the melody was not a familiar one. Now and then this fatherly voice ceased singing long enough to speak to the mother, calling her attention to the baby's charms.

If Clark had not been hungry he could have slept, notwithstanding the disturbance in the next room, for he was tired out. It was now past one o'clock, and he had had only a light six-o'clock supper. He became more and more wakeful, and also grew tired of the song, the same air having been kept up from the first without any variation; and although the baby varied the monotony by frequent and long-continued outbreaks, there was, nevertheless, a good deal of sameness to the concert. Clark soon knew that this baby was the first for that couple; for did n't he hear both father and mother declare, even while 't was yet madly howling, that there never was such a sweet little mite?

After the cry was ended the father seemed to be having a kind of frolic with the infant, and Clark heard the mother give the fond father a mild scolding for making the baby wakeful.

"This is n't becoming rested for the work of the morrow," thought Clark. Then he fell back on his bad habit of rhyming, with the following result:

OUR FIRST BABY.

And now we have a baby
  With little hands and feet,
And dimples, too. Ah, may be
  You think she is n't sweet!

Some babies make wry faces
  And gape most impolite,
These are but lovely graces
  With our dear little mite!

She makes tremendous music
  For such a little mouse;
Could any one abuse it
  For waking up the house?

> For babies cry at midnight,
>   Or in the early morn;
> Are hungry or don't *feel* right
>   E'en on the day they're born.
>
> They thus make known their ailing,
>   Their pains must be allayed;
> Instead of crossly railing,
>   They give a serenade.
>
> So sing, my little lady,
>   And let your wants be known;
> Whate'er the hour, my baby,
>   We'll heed your winsome tone.
>
> And when at night she calleth,
>   We'll rise, in white arrayed,
> To march with her who bawleth—
>   A strict *undress* parade!
>
> But when the wretched colic
>   Has been induced to flee,
> 'T is then we have our frolic
>   With little ba-bi-e.

Still, even after *this*, Clark felt no drowsiness come over him. He was too hungry to sleep. His watch told him it was now half-past two.

"I certainly can't sleep until I eat something. A few crackers would be better than nothing," thought Clark. In answer to his bell-call a boy came, and Clark gave him half a dollar, telling him to bring up some lunch if it was possible to procure any at that hour of the night. In the course of half an hour the boy returned bearing a tray on which were bread, butter, cold roast beef, and a glass of milk.

After this lunch Clark soon fell asleep, though the baby had had another spell, and the same crying, singing, and tramping were going on again.

Clark dreamed he was attending a baby-show and saw on exhibition four little baby sisters, all of the same age, and all crying at the same moment.

XV.

ALTHOUGH Clark had had a poor night's rest he was up as usual the following morning, and by nine o'clock went forth to call upon the Indianapolis buyers.

The commercial travellers whom he had met in Louisville had moved almost in a body to Indianapolis, and he called upon three firms in succession, only to find certain travellers had stolen a march upon him—having already engaged the attention of the buyers. Where he next called the buyer was occupied in reading the morning's mail. Clark introduced himself and said:

"I suppose you will be busy for a while with your mail?"

"Yes, I am late to-day,—but I shall soon be at liberty, and I'm glad to see you. Take a chair and make yourself at home."

Clark accepted the invitation to be seated, and occupied himself in reading the newspaper.

In the course of half an hour the buyer was ready to look at Clark's samples of keels, and Clark had just begun quoting prices when another salesman came in.

"I beg your pardon, Mr. Clark, but I had forgotten that I had an engagement at this hour with this gentleman. Can you call about eleven?"

"Certainly," said Clark.

He once again went the rounds of the other stores, and found the buyers engaged as before with other travellers.

He called to keep his eleven o'clock engagement, but the buyer was not in the office. A clerk informed Clark that the person wanted was at present engaged in selling a bill of goods but would soon be at liberty—so Clark waited until nearly noon, when the buyer appeared and said:

"Now, Mr. Clark, we can talk business. It is a shame to have kept you so long, but I had a customer."

Clark again displayed his samples, and was rehearsing what to him had become during the past week a kind of stereotyped speech about

" quality" and other favorable points concerning his keels, when another batch of letters came in.

" Will you excuse me if I just glance over these letters?"

Clark of course assented, and there was a further delay of half an hour.

Another opportunity came to Clark to repeat his little speech about "quality," etc., when a clerk came to tell the buyer there was a lady at the door in a carriage waiting to see him.

" I will not be away over five minutes," said the buyer. It was fully a quarter of an hour before Clark again had the chance to speak his little piece about quality, etc.,—but he had only recited a part of it before the buyer said: "I am sorry to interrupt you again, but it is my dinner hour. I would be glad to have you dine with me."

As the invitation was evidently given with the wish that it should be accepted, Clark accompanied the buyer home and had a very good dinner. The buyer was very agreeable company, too, and his wife equally so.

Clark and the buyer returned to the store and renewed their discussion over prices, quality, etc., but there were still so many interruptions that Clark did not take his order until after four o'clock, and then it was for a very moderate quantity of goods.

He did not succeed in doing any thing elsewhere, for the different buyers still remained occupied with certain travellers.

"I really ought to remain in Indianapolis another day—but I want to have my trip over as soon as possible. Besides, there are so many competitors here I think I may as well resign. It reminds me of one day when I went fishing for trout in a small brook where the fish were scarce, but I found anglers without number ahead of me."

XVI.

CLARK returned to the hotel about six o'clock with the intention of packing, and going to Terre Haute in the evening. On the way to his room, and when passing the parlor, he was surprised to see an old friend whom he had not met for years.

" Why, Fred Clark ! "

" Tom Park ! "

Never were two friends more glad to meet each other.

Tom Park was an Episcopal clergyman. He was of the same age as Clark, and they had been to school together, and afterward to college, graduating in the same class. Tom Park, who had married since Clark had seen him, now introduced his wife, also his sister, a young lady of twenty. Tom had recently resigned his parish in Kentucky and accepted a call to another in New York State. They were now on their way to Chicago, where they expected to spend a few days before their departure East. They would be in Indianapolis until the following evening.

Tom said to Clark: "We are going from Chicago to Buffalo by steamer around the Lakes. Why can't you make the trip with us?"

Clark explained the situation, how that he was on a business trip, and must do his best to complete it as soon as possible, and so return to his regular duties at the office.

Clark and the Parks had separated to prepare for supper, and Clark was in his room thinking how good it seemed to meet an old, tried friend in a strange land. He took up his violin and had played a few moments when he heard a piano. Some one was playing one of Beethoven's sonatas most beautifully. Clark's violin became silent at once. He opened his door so that he might hear the pianist better. "I never heard any one play with so much feeling. It is beautiful," said Clark to himself as he stepped out into the hall. Then, almost unconsciously, and still holding his violin and bow, he walked on until near the door of the room wherein was the cause of his enchantment. There he stood, when, without warning, the door flew open and he was confronted by Tom Park, who said: " You here, Fred ? I was just going to call you for supper." Then, as Clark did not move, Tom added : " Are you asleep ? "

" Oh," said Clark, apparently just coming to himself, " I was listening to that music."

" We are in luck," said Tom. " The landlord's family, who are now East, usually occupy these rooms, and we have been invited to make ourselves at home and use the piano. It is a new instrument, and my sister is happy."

As they entered the room Clara Park was rising from the piano, but upon Clark's invitation she resumed her playing.

Tom soon interrupted the music with " Beg your pardon, Fred. You have brought your wife, I see. Mrs. Clark, let me introduce you to my wife and sister." Tom had taken the violin from Clark, and was now holding it toward the ladies, who bowed and expressed gratification at meeting one of whom they had often heard.

" I would like very much to hear your wife sing. Probably, like most singers, she would prefer to use her voice now rather than right after supper," said Clara Park.

"Tom has told me about a little song you play especially for your children. Could n't you play it now?" said Mrs. Park.

Clark played the hymn for the first time since he had stood before the picture on the day of his departure from New York. Again the little child's voice came from the violin, and the other little voices joined in. When he had finished, Clark saw a tear trickling down Clara Park's cheek, and he thought :

"That is the highest compliment my children's voices ever had."

Clark decided to remain in Indianapolis until noon the following day.

"I shall still arrive at Terre Haute in plenty of time to attend to business, and leave for St. Louis to-morrow night. Tom is a good fellow, and it would seem heathenish to go away to-night, when we have not seen each other before for so long. I shall lose no time. Tom is a good fellow. We can talk over old times." These were Clark's thoughts as he went to bed.

The first thing Clark did the following morning after dressing was to pack his trunk and valise.

"Now I shall have nothing to do before train-time but visit with Tom and talk over old times. Tom is such a good, whole-souled fellow!"

After breakfast there was more piano and violin music than was consistent with Clark's desire to talk over old times with Tom, and Clark changed his mind about taking the noon train for Terre Haute.

"I'll stay to-day," he said to himself. "What is the loss of one day? I have not seen Tom before for years. Tom is a royal good fellow. It seems unfriendly to even think of leaving him in such haste. I'll remain here until to-night."

So he stayed, parting with the Parks late that night, and feeling sorry business compelled him to go even then.

When he was on the cars, bound for Terre Haute, it occurred to him that he had not had much conversation with Tom, nor talked over old times, after all. He felt a trifle guilty when he thought of this, but wound up with:

"Tom is a good fellow. I hope we shall meet again soon. We can then talk over old times."

XVII.

CLARK arrived at Terre Haute at about midnight. He was no sooner in bed than the mosquitoes attacked him. There was no netting over the bed, and for a while, notwithstanding he slapped right and left, the pests had a very good time. Finally, Clark rang the bell. The clerk answered it in person.

"Have n't you any mosquito-netting for the protection of your guests?" asked Clark.

"Yes, I can find you a piece; but this is the first complaint we have had about mosquitoes in this hotel."

"I suppose so! But at the other hotel, a block away, the mosquitoes are terrible, and fly away with the guests' baggage," said Clark, who was in a sarcastic mood, and very sleepy, too.

The netting was brought, but proved to be too small to cover the bed, and Clark experimented with the material some time without making a success of it. He was even inclined to believe the mosquitoes were laughing at his efforts. At last he deserted the bed and arranged the netting over a high-back lounge pretty successfully. Now, Clark soon discovered that a five-foot sofa did not make a comfortable bed for a person six feet long. He arose, placed a chair at the foot of the sofa, and tried it again.

"That is n't bad!" he thought.

But the mosquitoes seemed determined upon giving Clark no rest; and although they did not get at him for a while, yet the netting was so low they could fly close to his head and sing. He had never before heard such loud mosquito voices. Had they sung in good tune and together, it would have been very sweet; but alas! it was all discord. He could not recognize any particular air, though he was quite positive one old fellow was trying to sing that familiar strain :

> "We 're going to hum till morning,
> We 're going to hum till morning,
> We 're going to hum till morning,
>   Till daylight doth appear!"

Suddenly Clark felt a bite! Yes! one scoundrel had found a hole in the netting, come in, and drawn blood. As Clark's slap hurt only himself and did not touch the too-lively mosquito, he arose, lighted the gas, and drove the villain out. Then he again arranged the netting, crawled under, and thought rather sadly:

> " Who comes to me when I 'm in bed,
> And buzzes 'round my tired head,
> And never stops till blood is shed?
> Mosquito!
>
> " Who, when I think my net is tight,
> Creeps in a little hole at night,
> And welcomes me with sting and bite?
> Mosquito!"

He fell asleep finally, thinking of the Parks and the pleasant time he had in their company. But he did not sleep long, for a dog's loud barking in the yard, under the window, soon awakened him. Another dog answered dog number one; number three joined in, and another, and another, and still another added their several barks, until it seemed as though the whole population of canines had awoke to give the full moon a grand serenade. Clark heard a clock strike two, and afterward, at the end of what seemed a very long hour, three, and then the dog in the yard concluded to set the others a good example and go to bed. Clark, too, dropped off, his last thoughts being :

"I shall not be obliged to rise early, for there are only two houses to call on here, and I don't leave for St. Louis till night."

Poor Clark! At five o'clock he was wide awake again. The cause—the running of one of the noisiest of sewing-machines in the room directly overhead. Becoming accustomed to this, he was again losing himself when a piano struck up in the room across the hall. Somebody not at all advanced in music was practising the scales very slowly but with much power!

"I declare! This *is* a scaly place for sleeping," thought Clark, as he arose. It was half-past six. By seven he had dressed, and was improvising upon his violin when a loud knock on the door connecting his room with the next startled him. A man's voice called out gruffly:

"I say, mister, just give us a rest with that old fiddle. I did n't get to bed till late, and want to sleep. Or, if you must scrape the miserable old thing, 'spose you let up on the tune the old cow died on and give us a jig or something lively."

Clark put his violin aside without a word, but he mused:

"To think that, after being kept awake nearly all night, some one should object to my violin at seven in the morning!"

He had breakfast, and called early upon the only two jobbers in his line of goods. The buying partner of one of these firms was East, and would not be at home for several weeks. The buyer for the other house was also absent, but was expected that noon; so Clark had four hours before him to spend as best he could. He went wandering about the city until he stumbled on the Wabash River.

"Why, what an idiot I am! Here is a river, and I have wasted at least half an hour which might have been passed in fishing," he thought.

"Are there any fish worth catching in this stream?" he inquired of a man who was repairing a boat.

"Millions of them! Lots of black-bass. Can catch a boat-load in an hour or two."

"Where can I hire a boat?"

"I'm your man for that."

"Have you bait and fishing tackle?"

"Yes, plenty."

Clark was soon fishing. The man had told him a reasonable kind of a lie, considering fish was the subject, for on that topic no one is ever suspected of telling the exact truth. There were not boat-loads of bass to be taken, and they did'nt come about the boat crying to be caught, but in the course of time Clark had a bite, and pulled in a small sun-fish. The next bite was different, and Clark landed a four-pound bass.

"I would rather take a fish like this than any order for goods ever given!" exclaimed the enthusiastic fisherman.

He soon forgot all about business, and fished until his bait gave out, and then for the first time looked at his watch.

"Three o'clock! Whew! I have been at it six hours."

He had a good string of bass, and the owner of the boat was evidently surprised when Clark returned with them.

"You don't mean to tell me you caught all those yourself?"

"Of course, I did. There lack a few of being a *boat-load*, but I am very well satisfied."

These fish Clark presented to the proprietor of the hotel, with the request that they be cooked for supper. He then ate a cold dinner and hurried off to see the buyer who had been expected back at noon. This individual had not returned, but had telegraphed he should be detained two or three days longer.

"The express for St. Louis does not leave until after midnight. I'll have an hour or two more bassing," thought Clark.

He fished faithfully and with fair success until the sun went down, when the bass ceased biting. Then he gave it up and departed for St. Louis very much pleased with his visit to Terre Haute. In fact, he considered it had been by far the most successful day of his trip.

XVIII.

HE had a lower berth on the sleeping-car, and commenced well enough, soon falling asleep; but he awoke before long, and heard loud talking outside the car. The train had come to a standstill, and Clark soon gathered that there was a freight train off the track right ahead, which had blocked the road.

One voice said:

"There will be several hours' delay, and perhaps we shall be here all night. Let's get a berth."

"All right! So say I."

Two men now came into the car and asked the porter for sleeping accommodations—"A place to roost," they said.

They were bound for a point at which the train was due at three in the morning, and so had not taken a berth at the start, but now that there was a prospect of being out all night, they wanted "a place to roost."

All the lower berths were taken, and the two men comprising the roosting party were given the berth over Clark.

They had clubbed together, and were to make this one berth do for their two large, heavy bodies. Clark felt uncomfortable about having those two big men over him. It seemed very probable the fastenings sustaining the upper berth might give way under such weight, and occupants and all be precipitated upon him. After the two had climbed up things did creak fearfully, and Clark's hands were raised to ward off the anticipated fall. No such catastrophe came to pass, however. But Clark could not sleep, for whenever the men above him turned over or moved, there was a groaning and a creaking unpleasant to Clark's ears. Soon the two men began quarrelling about room.

"Keep on your own side."

"I am."

"No, you ain't. You've more than your share."

"I have n't!"

"You have!"

"You're another!"

"Look here! If it was n't for making a row I 'd just pitch you out of this bunk!"

"Try it, if you think best."

Here the porter came and told them they would have to keep quiet; that they would disturb the passengers.

After this they quarrelled in lower tones, but Clark heard all they said, and several times thought there was really going to be a fight.

The car became warmer the longer it stood still, and as Clark could not sleep, he decided to dress and go out for some fresh air.

He walked to the scene of the wreck, and there saw the engine on its side and a number of freight cars badly broken up. He learned there was no one injured, though there had been several narrow escapes.

The engineer and fireman had saved themselves by jumping before the engine had turned over. Clark stood viewing the wreck, when he heard a bell ring.

"I verily believe my train is backing!" said Clark to himself. He was hurrying back to his car when one of the workmen said:

"You can't catch it. They are going to Terre Haute, where they will breakfast."

"How far is it to Terre Haute?"

"Four miles or thereabouts."

Four miles was not much of a walk for Clark under ordinary circumstances, but it was a gloomy kind of a night, and dense woods lined each side of the track. There was a high wind, too, with an occasional drop of rain. A hand-car stood on the track, and Clark said to one of the men:

"I'll pay you five dollars if you will take me back to the train."

"Can't do it unless the boss says so."

"Where is he?"

"That's him," pointing to a tall man.

Clark approached the boss and said: "I belong on the sleeping-car bound for St. Louis, and"—

"Why did n't you stay there? You don't do any good here—that's a sure case."

"Well, I *am* here, having left the car thinking the train would stay here till the track was cleared; and I would like to get back."

"Easy enough. You've got legs!" And the men laughed.

"Can't you let one of these men take me back in this hand-car?"

"Not much! Plenty of work here. Can give you a job, too, if you want one."

It now began raining quite heavily, and Clark was muttering : " What a scrape ! " He stood under the lee of one of the freight cars to keep out of the wet, but the water began dripping off on him, so he moved his head-quarters to a tree, under which he stood for half an hour or longer, still muttering " What a scrape ! "

Soon there was a lull in the rain, and he started to walk to Terre Haute. Striking a match, he found it was three o'clock. To add to his other discomforts, he was very hungry. He walked rapidly, and was well on his journey, when the rain set in again harder than before. Seeing a dim light near by, he ran toward it, coming abruptly against a barbed wire-fence, which astonished him a good deal, and pricked him too, but his clothes were not torn.

He felt his way now until he found an opening, and then came to a log-house wherein a candle was burning. He knocked.

"Who's there?" asked a man's voice.

"A gentleman."

"Nice time of night for a gentleman to be prowling about. Bet you're a tramp."

Clark explained how it was he happened to be there.

"All right! I'll let you in. You talk like an honest man; but if you try to go back on me 't will be the worse for you, and don't you forget it!"

The man opened the door and Clark entered.

"Do you want a place to stretch yourself?"

"No, I thank you. I will not lie down, for as soon as the rain ceases I mean to walk back to the train. I think it will clear up soon, for I had a glimpse of the moon a minute ago."

"No need of going back to Terre Haute. When they have cleared the track your train will come along. My son is a railroad man, and I'll have him flag it to make a sure thing of it. It is a long three miles to Terre Haute. Lie down and make yourself comfortable. Excuse my taking you for a tramp."

"Oh, that is all right. I feel like one. Could you give me some bread? I am very hungry."

"Can give you bread, butter, and sausage."

"Thank you. Bread and butter will be sufficient."

This repast tasted very well, and after it he lay down and slept till seven o'clock, at which hour his host aroused him and said the track was clear, and that the train would soon come along. Clark paid for his bread and butter and lodging—for which the man would take only twenty-five cents,—and was glad when he was once more on the Pullman sleeping-car. It was past noon that Sunday when the train arrived at St. Louis. As Clark had had nothing but bread and butter since supper the day before, he was almost famished; so before going to the hotel he had dinner at the Union Depôt dining-hall. He had telegraphed for a room, but not having put in an appearance with the rest of the belated travellers the clerk had given the room set apart for him to another person, and Clark was forced to take a small room on the top floor, the hotel being very full.

Clark had his trunk sent up, and was once again playing on his violin. But he was not as well satisfied with its tone as he usually was.

"You are not in as good voice as you were in Indianapolis. I suppose you miss your piano accompaniment. So do I. Tom is a good fellow."

XIX.

AT the hotel Clark had found a letter from Morgan headed "Aboard the *Fleetwing*." It made him homesick.

Morgan had written that he felt as well as ever, and was having a glorious time.

In the evening Clark went to church. As he was walking down the middle aisle, after the close of the service, he saw on the other side of the church a person whom he recognized.

There's Ed Hartley large as life, and considerably larger," thought Clark.

Yes, there was no mistaking Ed, though Clark had not seen him for ten years.

Ed had grown stout or been blown up—that was all the change in him.

Clark would have known his old friend anywhere, by the twinkle of Ed's eyes.

They seemed to have the power of seeing into every thing, and through any thing—and yet they were not sharp nor staring; but bright, playful, eyes with a never-failing twinkle. Clark, the poet, never saw them without thinking:

> " Twinkle, twinkle, little eye,
> How I wonder what you spy,
> All around, in every nook,
> Shining with a playful look ! "

The two friends met in the vestibule.

" Why, you old reprobate ! "

That was the very churchly greeting Clark received, and which, perhaps, shocked some of the more staid members of the departing congregation.

" Fred, this is my wife."

" Where's yours ? " he asked, scarcely giving Clark a chance to pay his respects to Mrs. Hartley.

"I have none," replied Clark.

" Just what I was afraid of. But I know a widow who will just suit you. You are too old to think of marrying any thing different. Come along home with me and we'll compare notes for the past ten years, and see who has had the most fun. We live three miles away, and you must stay all night. I'll lend you every thing you need, except a tooth brush ! "

They drove out, and Clark found his friend pleasantly situated in a very homelike, roomy, house. Ed Hartley was one of St. Louis' rising young lawyers—not that he was fond of rising early in the morning; far from it.

"There are two little cherubs asleep up-stairs," said Ed. "Ah! Fred, you bachelors don't half live, after all. But, by the by, I started to tell you about that widow. To begin with, she has five children. Now, when a man puts off the *great event* until he is as advanced in years as you are, there is nothing like marrying a widow with perquisites in the shape of a lot of children. It places him on an equal footing with those of us who have been for some time family-men. Still, you were always a rather conscientious fellow at school, and I shall be shocked if, after marrying the widow, you try to pass yourself off for a genuine, simon-pure family-man. Credit to whom credit is due! By all means have a portrait, life-size, of the widow's late husband hung up in the parlor. Have it labelled: 'The Husband of my Youth.'"

Of all talkers and teasers ever born, Ed Hartley was at the head. Mrs. Hartley was of a decidedly retiring disposition ; but, as Ed was so much the reverse, the couple made a good average. After Ed had run the widow-subject in the ground and they were all seated in the cosy study, Clark asked :

"Whom do you think I met in Indianapolis?"

"Give it up."

"Tom Park."

"Tom Park? Bless him! Has he settled there?"

"No; he resigned his parish somewhere in Kentucky, and is now on his way to another in New York State. He is to be in Chicago a few days, and then he goes East around the Lakes by steamer. Tom is a good fellow."

"Was he alone? or is he married?"

"His wife and sister were with him."

"Ah! Now you 've hit it!" said Ed; "it is the *sister* we want to hear about."

Now, it is no disgrace for a man of thirty-five, or even twice thirty-five, to blush ; and so we record it here that Clark blushed then and there.

"I thought so!" said those dancing eyes which seemed to go all through Clark. He felt very much as a timid witness might who was about to be cross-examined.

"Is she pretty?" asked Ed.

"She is handsome."

"Ah! I thought so," again seemed to say those eyes, and Clark knew he was blushing again.

"How old is she?"

"Twenty."

"Is she accomplished and bright?"

"Decidedly."

"You are thirty-four or five, are you not?"

"Thirty-five."

"Twenty from thirty-five leaves how much?"

"Fifteen."

"Right! You are a lightning calculator! Now, fifteen is about the right difference under the circumstances. A man of twenty-five would hardly be justified in marrying a girl of ten, but twenty and thirty-five is n't bad!"

Ed ran on in this strain some time, but at last changed the subject and talked over old times. Mrs. Hartley made an attentive audience, and took much interest in the experiences and scrapes of the two school-boys. It was past eleven before they thought of bed.

"Don't worry if we don't call you early," said Ed, "for the truth is we have been going through the servant ordeal lately. Our tenth within six months came highly recommended, and has just departed, carrying away enough spoons to start a store. Like several other girls who left us suddenly, she said her mother was sick! We don't know where her mother lives. Probably the spoons were needed for giving medicine! We have been running this ranche ourselves for a few days—also the range, which is the most obstinate thing I ever had to cross-examine. Sometimes we have breakfast at nine, oftener at ten; but to-morrow I'll get up early—say eight o'clock—and stir up the range, etc., so that you can have an early breakfast, as you are here on business."

Clark was in one of his wakeful moods. According to all good usage, he should have been sleepy after such a night as the previous one; but he was n't. "Tom is a good fellow," he thought. "Now, if I had gone to Chicago with him, done my business there, and come back here, it would have given me some pleasant hours with him. Tom is a good fellow, for a fact."

Then Clark tried to think of other things, but failed to concentrate his thoughts upon any thing not connected with *Tom.*

"It would be an easy matter to go to Chicago to-morrow night and come back here a few days hence. Tom is a good fellow. Chicago is a very important place. The sooner I go there and look after the interests of our house, the better. I'll leave St. Louis to-morrow night and come back after finishing Chicago."

There was something in this resolution which seemed to give Clark peace, for he fell asleep and did not awake until Ed knocked at his door.

"It is nine o'clock. Breakfast in half an hour. How did you sleep?"

"Very well indeed, after I got at it."

"Did the babies disturb you?"

"No; I did n't hear them."

"Then you *must* have slept! I have the two noisiest infants ever born. One is a boy, the other a girl; so we have named them the hub-*bub* and the cri-*sis.* Of whom did you dream last night—the widow or Tom's sister?"

"Neither."

At breakfast the Hartleys proposed sending to the hotel for Clark's baggage, supposing he would be in the city several days; they were therefore surprised when he told them he was to leave for Chicago that evening.

"You surely can't transact your business in St. Louis in one day?" queried Ed.

"No; but I intend returning here after finishing Chicago."

"Is n't that a little out-of-the-way manner of doing things? I don't pretend to be a business man, and I know Tom is a good fellow! but is n't it just a little out of the usual course, so to speak, as it were, in a manner, as aforesaid?"

Ed's eyes were dancing again, and Clark was blushing, but Mrs. Hartley considerately changed the subject and looked hard at Ed. Clark was spared until the time came for saying good-bye; then Ed said:

"Tom is a good fellow, Clark. Remember me to him to-morrow. When you return to St. Louis this week come right here, bag and baggage. Did I understand you to say Tom was going around the Lakes by steamer from Chicago?"

"Yes."

"Of course you will not make the Lake trip with him?"

"Certainly not. I have not the time. Business is business."

"And you are really coming back here in a few days?"

"Most assuredly."

"What do you want to bet on it?"

"Why, if I was in the habit of betting, I'd wager any thing. I *must* come back to attend to my business here."

"Of course you must! But Tom is a good fellow! Good-bye, Fred."

"What a queer chap Ed is," thought Clark. "He must torment even a judge in court half to death sometimes. I don't see any thing strange in my running on to Chicago to see Tom. He will probably start on his journey around the Lakes by Thursday. I shall have a pleasant visit with him, staying at the same hotel; then I can return to St. Louis, and finish here. Of course I shall, while in Chicago, attend to business during the day, and be with Tom evenings. As the journey to and from

Chicago will be made at night I don't see that I shall lose any time at all. We have a good run of customers in Chicago, and the sooner, I look after them the better. Tom is a good fellow."

That Clark did not quite succeed in satisfying himself that leaving St. Louis was exactly business-like was evident from the fact that he repeated the arguments in favor of his doing so over and over again, during the day. Indeed, he spent more time in arguing to satisfy his mind, than he did talking up his goods to the buyers; and he made no sales. He saw nearly all the leading firms, however, and told them he was going to Chicago that night, but would return to St. Louis within a few days. As he stepped aboard the train he thought: "Tom is a good fellow. We'll talk over old times. Chicago is an important place. I am glad I decided to go there without delay to look after our trade. Tom *is* a good fellow."

XX.

CLARK arrived in Chicago about eight o'clock the following morning. He had not slept well. After going to the hotel at which the Parks were staying he took a room, made himself presentable, and then sent up his card to Tom. The Parks were just on the point of going to breakfast when the card was brought in, and a look of surprise came over the face of each of them.

The Parks and Clark had breakfast together, and soon afterward Clark said to Tom : " Now I must go to work. We shall have all the evening together, and can then talk over old times. I wish I was a 'gentleman of leisure,' but unfortunately I am a commercial traveller for the time being, and must stick to my text— which I hope you always do. What a day this would be for a sail on the lake. But business says ' stay ashore and be a landlubber.' Tom, has living inland for five years made you lose your love for the water and yachting ? "

"Not by a long shot. I made up my mind to never again accept a call to any parish which was located away from the sea. To begin with, I always found I could write better sermons in a boat or in sight of the ocean than anywhere else."

"I wish Tom would take a floating chapel; it would just suit him," said Mrs. Park.

"Oh, it would n't do at all," said Clara Park, "for he would soon have a mast and sail rigged up instead of a spire, and be cruising around while service was going on."

Boating now became the topic in earnest, and Clark found he was in the company of very enthusiastic sailors.

"Why should n't we have a sail this morning on Lake Michigan?" asked Clark, forgetting about business entirely. All favored the plan strongly, and by ten o'clock they were at the lake-front inspecting boats. There were numerous small sailing craft for hire, none of which were very pleasing, however. Clark now caught sight of a sloop-rigged yacht anchored off from shore a short distance. It was a trim little vessel with long spars, and looked as though she might be a good sailer.

"Who is the owner of that yacht?" asked Clark of a man who was fishing successfully for perch.

"Captain Hicks; he is aboard now."

"Does he let her?"

"He takes out parties."

Tom remained with the ladies while Clark looked up a row-boat and rowed off to the yacht to interview Captain Hicks. The captain told Clark he never let the *Wanderer* go unless he went himself, and he could n't go that day.

"We can manage her all right, and I will be responsible for any damage done," said Clark.

"But you are a stranger to me," replied the captain, smiling.

Clark persevered until the captain said: "If you can convince me that you and the other gentleman are able seamen you can have the *Wanderer* for a dollar an hour. I tell you what 't is—you bring your party aboard, and if you can get the yacht under way in good, seamanship style you can take her."

"All right," said Clark, and forthwith brought the Parks aboard.

Captain Hicks was soon convinced that the

Wanderer was in good hands, and he rowed ashore in his own boat, taking in tow the one Clark had been using.

The breeze was rather light when they started out, and Clark set the gaff-topsail.

"It seems good to be on a yacht once more," said Tom.

"I wish it would blow a little harder. Tom is never satisfied until the rail is under water," said Mrs. Park.

"No raillery, please," said Tom.

She has a jib-topsail; why not put it on her?" came from Clark.

"Aye, aye, sir," cried Tom.

Clark went out on the end of the bowsprit and unfurled the jib-topsail.

"How does it seem out there?" inquired Tom.

"Like being at home again. I remember we thought it great fun to go out on the old *Ida's* bowsprit when the waves were so high that we were wet through and through. But I'm not exactly rigged for such an adventure to-day."

The jib-topsail was soon drawing finely.

When Clark came aft they all called for some music from his violin which he had brought aboard with him. The wind was blowing harder now, and Tom was as happy as a clam at high water.

"This is glorious," he exclaimed, "I feel as though I could preach a fair kind of a sermon!"

"Oh, don't think of it!" came in chorus.

"Tom's favorite texts are about the sea; and once when he was speaking *extempore* he became excited over his own description of one of St. Paul's voyages, and made us laugh by telling us the apostle had a splendid cruise!" said Clara Park.

"We shall be obliged to take in our topsails. Those vessels to windward have a stiff breeze," said Clark.

The light sails were soon furled, and as the wind had increased very much the *Wanderer* had all the canvas she could carry comfortably, and her "crew" sat up to windward.

"There is really no excuse for upsetting a boat," said Tom. "It all comes from carrying more sail than there is any excuse for doing. I once knew a professional tease who was continually upsetting persons because he had a morbid curiosity for seeing how much they would stand without being upset! It is a good deal the same with a boat."

"Is this the commencement of the sermon?" asked Clark.

"There's a boat upset!" cried Mrs. Park.

"Where?"

"Ahead of us a short distance."

"Mrs. Park was right—not a quarter of a mile away two persons were seen clinging to the bottom of a small boat.

"We must pick them up," said Clark. "There is a woman there. I will go forward, Tom, and you luff up when we are near them and I'll take in the jib."

Tom made a good "come to," and the *Wanderer* was soon along-side of the wrecked boat.

Clark was helping to get the woman aboard when she cried :

"O my child! my child!"

"Take care of my violin, Tom," said Clark, as he removed coat, vest, and shoes in a twinkling.

He had discovered the child, still buoyed up

by its clothes, some distance away, and had pulled the woman aboard, removed the articles mentioned, and was overboard in less time than it takes to write it. Clark was a good swimmer, but the water was rough, and several times he lost sight of the child. When at last he had it in his grasp it seemed lifeless. He held its head above the water, and then the child after gasping for breath commenced crying lustily.

"I never thought I could be so glad to hear a child cry! I was n't a moment too soon, though," thought Clark. He was soon picked up by the *Wanderer*, and upon getting aboard looked at once for his violin. It was safe.

The wrecked boat was taken in tow, and the yacht headed for the harbor. Clark was fairly embraced by the father and mother of the child he had saved. It could not be called a warm embrace, for they were all too wet!

At first Clark had had a sort of contempt for the father, who had made no effort to save his own child, but when he saw that the man had but one arm and stated that he could not swim a stroke, Clark thought better of him.

As the yacht rounded-to at her anchorage, Captain Hicks came out to meet the party, and took them all ashore. The family who had been upset lived near the water, and tried to persuade Clark to go with them and put on dry clothes, but there being a hack near by he called to the driver, and he, with the Parks, were taken to the hotel, and Tom loaned Clark a pair of pantaloons which were too short by four or five inches.

A drying and pressing at a tailor's brought Clark's out all right, and in the course of three hours he was clothed and in his right size.

When they were all together again that afternoon, Tom said to Clark:

"Fred, I want to ask you a question."

"Go ahead."

"Aside from the pleasure it gave you to save a human life, did n't you rather enjoy that swim?"

"Yes, I confess I did, after the child's cry told me 't was all right."

"I thought so, you water-dog. You looked as though you liked it, for you had a broad grin on your face!"

"I was very anxious about one thing, though," said Clark.

"What was that?"

"My violin. I was afraid some one would, in the excitement, smash it. The water was pretty cold; but while I was swimming about there, the thought that some one might sit down on my violin sent a shiver through me which made the water feel hot in comparison!"

XXI.

CLARK had transacted no business on this, his first day in Chicago, but he made himself a kind of half-way promise to work hard the following day. When morning came, however, he felt in any thing but a business humor. After breakfast he proposed that they should all take a drive, and they rode out to Lincoln Park.

In the afternoon they were on board the *Wanderer* again.

"What is the loss of one or two days?" Clark argued to himself. "I am having a good time with Tom, and may as well enjoy myself. Tom is a good fellow. We will talk over old times.

As Clark and Tom were fond of rowing, they indulged in a little moderate pulling in the evening, taking two small skiffs. Of course, the ladies could not be left behind, so Mrs. Park went with Tom and Clara Park with

Clark. Undoubtedly it was very severe upon Clark to be thus separated from Tom for a while, but he bore it bravely.

When Clark awoke on the morning of his fourth day in Chicago, he appeared to realize, for the first time, that he had been acting very unlike himself of late. His time had been devoted to—Tom during three entire days, when he should have been doing his utmost to act the part of a commercial traveller and push for orders. He knew, too, that his services were required at the office, and that nothing should have been allowed to interfere with the completion of his trip as soon as possible.

He now lectured himself unsparingly for even thinking of making the Lake trip, for, the truth was, he had thought seriously of going with the Parks on the steamer, after all.

"I will see the Chicago trade to-day. To-morrow Tom will leave on the steamer. Tom is a good fellow, and I would like to make the Lake trip with him, but of course it is not to be thought of. Business is business!"

Thus reasoned Clark, as he thought of the three days he had passed in Chicago.

After breakfast, he told Tom he was going to work that day, and then he went to his room to get his samples of keels. The samples seemed like strangers to him. As he was going out to make his first business call he hesitated.

"How unfriendly it would be for me to devote this day to business, when it is probably the last time Tom and I shall be together for a long while! Tom is a good fellow. We have n't talked over old times yet, either."

The samples were put back in the trunk, and Lake Michigan again smiled on the party.

Late that afternoon, when Clark was alone in his room, he stood before the glass gazing at himself—not admiringly, but with threatening aspect. Indeed, he was actually shaking his fist at his own reflection!

"Promise me one thing, old boy, and that is that you will leave for Milwaukee to-night. I would n't trust you if you remained over till to-morrow."

The promise came hard, but it was extracted at last, Clark shaking hands with his reflection to bind the agreement.

He surprised his friends by bidding them good-bye and departing on the 9 P. M. train for Milwaukee. As he had not said a word to any of them about going, this leave-taking was certainly very sudden, and Tom could not understand why Clark would not wait until morning and so see them off on the steamer.

Clark was on the train. The night was very pleasant and calm, but Clark's condition was not in keeping therewith, for within him all was very tempestuous. Old Probabilities would have hoisted the danger signal over him.

But as the train rushed on toward Milwaukee he complimented himself upon his "will-power."

"I am thankful I had the *will* to give up the crazy idea of that trip around the Lakes. Now I shall be able to attend to my business in Milwaukee, return to Chicago, finish there, and then take in St. Louis. Yes, I am glad I went away to-night."

The next moment he was very sorry.

When the train was well on toward Milwaukee he asked the conductor: "Is there a train going back to Chicago this evening?"

"No, sir."

"That's fortunate!" he thought, and immediately afterward, "I'm very sorry!" adding aloud: "There's consistency for you!" which remark caused a number of passengers to stare at him. Again he questioned the conductor, and was told there was a train leaving Milwaukee for Chicago at four in the morning, which was due in Chicago at 7 A. M. Clark would arrive at Milwaukee about midnight.

"Of course it is nonsense to think of that four-o'clock train," mused Clark.

When he arrived at Milwaukee he went to the hotel and to bed, congratulating himself again upon his "will-power." It was settled now. By the time he should be breakfasting the steamer would have sailed with the Parks aboard. "Tom is a good fellow, and I would like to talk over old times with him, but business is business," he said, as he turned out the gas.

After tossing about in bed for some time he arose, struck a match, and looked at his watch.

"Half-past two! I ought to have been asleep long ago. Now for a good long nap before breakfast. I have n't slept well lately. Tom is a good fellow."

He lay quietly for a while, though wide-awake.

Again he jumped up and struck a match.

"Twenty minutes past three."

He touched the electric-bell button. A colored boy answered the call.

"Order the omnibus to wait for me. I'll be down in fifteen minutes or less. Am going to Chicago on the four-o'clock train."

At the depôt he sent a telegram to his partner, which read as follows: "Going around the Lakes. Home next week. Skipped St. Louis, Milwaukee, and Chicago," and he found himself writing "Tom is a good fellow!" which brought him to his senses.

"I'm terribly worked up and absent-minded. How hot 't is!"

The train was an hour late, so it was eight o'clock before Clark arrived at Chicago. He entered a hack, and, with his luggage, soon brought up at the steamer's dock.

The Parks were on the upper deck, and with astonishment saw him coming on board.

"I changed my mind, and am to be one of your party after all," he said.

* * * * *

Good-bye, Clark; you have ceased to be a commercial traveller, and so we leave you.

Tom is a good fellow, and you showed your great regard for him when you deserted your business so that you might join him on the Lake trip. You did not take very kindly to commercial travelling, but we know you have a very affectionate feeling for Indianapolis and Chicago, and also for the Lake steamer, upon whose deck you told Clara Park the "old, old, story," just as though you were imparting a bit of news; while, of course, the fact was, every one at all interested had discovered the truth long before.

We are a little surprised that any one who prides himself, as you do, upon being a good sailor, should feel obliged to call upon Tom to tie a knot for you.

You and Tom have not yet talked over old times together very much, but perhaps after the trip which you are soon to make, and which will be strictly non-commercial, you may give your neglected college-chum a little attention. Considering that you departed in haste from

St. Louis, so that you and Tom could meet and talk over old times ; neglected your business in Chicago for a like reason ; and astonished your partner by taking a pleasure trip on a Lake steamer, and all this so that you and Tom could be together and talk over old times ; we say, considering all these things, we cannot help thinking that you have been very neglectful of Tom.

Three months is a short engagement, Clark, and we feel certain you would have waited longer had you not longed for the time to come when, seated before your own hearthstone, and no longer a bachelor, you and Tom could talk over old times.

Tom is a good fellow !

THE END.

NEW BOOK PUBLICATIONS.

A Woman's Devotion; or, The Mixed Marriage. A story of the Rival Detectives. By JOHN W. POSTGATE. 12mo; 270 pages; paper..$ .35

Princess Andrea (Anselma); or, In Spite of All. Adapted from the French by ARTHUR D. HALL. This story is based upon the famous drama of VICTORIEN SARDOU. 12mo; 256 pages; paper..... .35

Called Back. By HUGH CONWAY. 12mo; paper; 228 pages; price.. .35

Chicago Sensations; or, Leaves from the Note-Book of a Chicago Reporter and Detective. Illustrated; 12mo; 154 pages; paper.. .25

Dark Days. By HUGH CONWAY. 12mo; 264 pages; paper............ .35

Fedora; or, The Tragedy in the Rue de la Paix. A most original, powerful and exciting French romance. Translated from the French of ADOLPH BELOT. Illustrated; 12mo, cloth; 303 pages; price, 35c in paper; in cloth.............................. 1.00

Fun Better Than Physic. By W. W. HALL, M. D. 12mo, cloth; 344 pages; price.. 1.00

Fast and Loose. By ARTHUR GRIFFITHS, author of "The Chronicles of Newgate." 12mo; 233 pages; paper.......................... .35

Prince Zilah, a Parisian Romance. Adapted from the French of JULES CLARETIE, by ARTHUR D. HALL. 12mo; 298 pages; paper. .35

Suppressed Sensations; or, Leaves from the Note-Book of a Chicago Reporter. Illustrated; 12mo, cloth; 254 pages; price 1.00

The Matapan Affair. From the French of FORTUNE DU BOISGOBEY. 12mo; 208 pages; paper.. .35

The Secret of Success; or, How to Get On in the World. By W. H. DAVENPORT ADAMS. 12mo, cloth; 388 pages............ 1.00

The Black Sorceress; a Tale of the Peasants' War. Adapted from the French of ALFRED DE BREHAT. Illustrated; 12mo; 200 pages; price, in paper, 35c; cloth............................. 1.00

The Executioner's Revenge. A story of the French Revolution. An intensely tragic romance. Translated from the French of LEONCE FERRET. 12mo, cloth; 313 pages; price, in paper, 35c; in cloth 1.00

The Gray and the Blue. A story founded on incidents connected with the War for the Union. By E. R. ROE. 12mo, cloth; 292 pages; price... 1.00

The Lakeside Musings. By TEN EYCK WHITE. 12mo, cloth; 300 pages.. 1.00

Was it a Murder; or, Who is the Heir? From the French of FORTUNE DU BOISGOBEY. 12mo, cloth; 341 pages; price, in paper, 35c; in cloth.. 1.00

West of the Missouri; Sketches and Stories of Frontier Life in the Old Times. By JAS. W. STEELE. 12mo, paper; 313 pages.. .35

Won at West Point; a Romance on the Hudson. A charming American story, marked by brilliancy of style, keenness of satire, frolicsome wit and mirth-provoking humor. By "FUSIL." 12mo, cloth; 300 pages.. 1.00

Woman's Work and Worth in Girlhood, Maidenhood and Wifehood. By W. H. DAVENPORT ADAMS. 12mo, cloth; 370 pages 1.00

Any of the above books sent, post-paid, on receipt of price, by

RAND, McNALLY & CO.,

323 Broadway, New York.   148-154 Monroe St., Chicago.

RAND, McNALLY & CO.'S POCKET MAPS OF FOREIGN COUNTRIES.

Afghanistan, see Persia .... $
Africa, mounted on rollers, 65 x 58 inches 18 00
Africa, in three sheets, two being 21 x 14 inches, and one 14 x 11 inches, and
   showing plans of cities of Algiers and Tunis 75
Alaska, 14 x 11 inches. Not kept in stock
Asia, mounted on rollers, 65 x 58 inches 18 00
Asia, 21 x 14 inches. Not kept in stock
Australia and New Zealand, with plans of Sydney and Pt. Jackson, 21x14 in 50
Austro-Hungarian Monarchy, with plan of Vienna, 21 x 14 inches 50
Belgium and The Netherlands, with plan of Brussels, 21 x 14 inches 50
British America (Dominion of Canada), 21 x 14 inches. Not kept in stock
Central America, 14 x 11 inches 50
China, 21 x 14 inches 50
Cuba, 21 x 14 inches 50
Denmark, with North portion of the German Empire, comprising Schles-
   wig Holstein and Lauenburg, 11 x 14 inches 50
England and Wales, 21 x 14 inches, with Index of cities, towns, etc. 75
Europe, 21 x 14 inches 50
Europe, mounted on rollers, 65 x 58 inches 18 00
France, 21 x 14 inches, with plan of Paris, and Index to cities, towns, etc. 75
Germany, in two sheets, 21x14 inches each, with Index to cities, towns, etc. 1 00
Greece, and the Ionian Islands, 21 x 14 inches 50
India, Indo-China and Further India, with plans of Calcutta and Bombay,
   21 x 14 inches 50
Ireland, 21 x 14 inches, with Index to cities, towns, etc. 75
Italy, 21 x 14 inches 50
Japan, in two sheets, 21 x 14 inches each 1 00
Mexico, 21 x 14 inches 50
Netherlands, see Belgium
New Zealand, see Australia
North America, mounted on rollers, 65 x 58 inches 18 00
North America, showing the West India Islands and Central America,
   21 x 14 inches. Not kept in stock
Palestine, with plans showing Environs of Jerusalem, journeyings of
   Christ, and sketch showing divisions into tribes, 21 x 14 inches.. 50
Persia and Afghanistan, 14 x 11 inches 50
Portugal, see Spain
Russia (European), 21 x 14 inches 50
Scotland, 21 x 14 inches, with Index to cities, towns, etc. 75
South America, mounted on rollers, 65 x 58 inches 18 00
South America, in two sheets, 21 x 14 inches, showing plans of Bay of Rio
   de Janeiro, Isthmus of Panama and City of Buenos Ayres 75
Spain and Portugal, with plans of Madrid and Lisbon, 21 x 14 inches 50
Sweden and Norway, 21 x 14 inches 50
Switzerland, 21 x 14 inches 50
Turkey in Asia (Asia Minor), and Transcaucasia, 21 x 14 inches 50
Turkey in Europe, 21 x 14 inches 50
World, on Mercator's Projection, 21 x 14 inches 50

   All of above pocket Maps are neatly bound in cloth cases.
   We make the production of maps a specialty, and keep the largest stock of map plates in the country. Are prepared to furnish Authors and Publishers with maps to illustrate Books of Travel and Historical and Educational Works at a merely nominal charge over the cost of paper and printing.
   Maps which require to be specially prepared, are compiled, engraved and printed with the utmost care and accuracy.
   A full line of Maps of the States and Territories in U. S. and of Foreign countries, on a *large scale;* also, of Modern Geographical, Classical, Political, Physical, Astronomical, Biblical, Anatomical and Biological Atlases, Globes and Map Racks, kept in stock.

                           RAND, McNALLY & CO., Publishers,

323 Broadway, NEW YORK.   148-154 Monroe St., CHICAGO.

Rand, McNally & Co.'s Map Publications.

Rand, McNally & Co.'s Indexed Atlas of the World. (Sold only by Subscription.)

Containing large scale maps of every Country and Civil Division upon the face of the Globe, together with historical, statistical and descriptive matter relative to each. Illustrated by colored diagrams, showing increase or decrease of population, wealth, debt and taxation, civil condition of people, chief productions, articles of manufacture and commerce, religious sects, etc. Accompanied by a new and original compilation, forming a ready-reference Index, which presents as its special feature, the arrangement in alphabetical order of nearly all known geographical names. In connection herewith is given the population of every city, town and village in the world that of the United States of America being taken from the census returns of 1880. 93 maps, 251 diagrams, 928 pages.

Rand, McNally & Co.'s Complete Business Atlas and Shippers' Guide. Price, $12.50; or $16.00 with Monthly Supplemental Changes.

Containing large scale maps of the Dominion of Canada, Old Mexico, Central America, Cuba, and the several States and Territories of the United States, together with a complete Reference Map of the World, printed in colors, accompanied by a new and original compilation and ready-reference Index, and accurately locating all cities, towns, post offices, railroad stations, villages, counties, parishes, islands, lakes, rivers, mountains, etc., showing in detail the entire Railroad System. The new and special features of this edition are: locating the branches of particular divisions of railroads upon which each station is located, the nearest mailing point of all local places, designating money-order offices, telegraph stations, and naming the Express Company doing business at the points where the several companies have offices, and the full census returns to date. 560 pages.

Rand, McNally & Co.'s New Railroad and County Map of the United States and Canada, mounted upon cloth, with rollers top and bottom, $15.00.

Compiled from the latest Government surveys, and drawn to an accurate scale. Size, 100 x 56 inches; scale, 32 miles to one inch; borders of States and Counties beautifully tinted, colors being printed from plates secured by letters patent. This work has occupied two years in compilation and engraving, at a cost of nearly $20,000; plates have been carefully corrected to date, presenting the finest work of Art of its kind. This Map is deserving of special mention as being the first map of the United States made upon a geometrical projection since the war.

Rand, McNally & Co.'s New Railroad and County Map, extending from the Atlantic Coast to the Western Boundary of Colorado.

Size, 70 x 56 inches, in colors, mounted upon heavy paper, rollers top and bottom (a section of our complete United States work); a map for the people at a popular price. Retail, $5.00; cloth, $8.00.

Rand, McNally & Co.'s New Railroad and County Map of the Western and Pacific Coast States and Territories, extending from the Western boundary of Indiana to the Pacific Coast.

Size, 66 x 56 inches, in colors, mounted upon heavy paper, rollers top and bottom (a section of our complete United States work). Retail, $5.00; mounted on cloth, $8.00.

Rand, McNally & Co.'s General Map of the Republic of Mexico.

Constructed from the best authorities, showing the completed and proposed Railways, Steamship routes and telegraphic communications, etc. Size, 72 x 52 inches; Price, mounted on rollers, varnished, $12.50; or, cut in sections and mounted on linen to fold in leather case, for portable use, $15.00.

Rand, McNally & Co.'s New Commercial Map of the United States and Canada.

Showing all the Counties, Railroads and Principal Towns up to date. It is eminently adapted both for school and office purposes. Size, 58 x 41 inches; scale, about sixty miles to one inch. Price, mounted on rollers, on heavy paper, $2.00; mounted on rollers, with cloth back, $3.50.

RAND, McNALLY & CO., Publishers,
Chicago and New York.

Rand, McNally & Co.'s
POCKET CYCLOPEDIA

A HAND-BOOK OF THINGS WORTH KNOWING.

Containing Tables, Rules, Practical Hints and Historical Sketches, for Farmers, Merchants, Mechanics, Bankers, Lawyers, Politicians, and the public generally, with

NUMEROUS COLORED DIAGRAMS

Illustrating some of the more important comparative statistics of the world.

This Cyclopedia gives more entertainment, instruction and valuable information per square inch of its pages than any other book ever published. The following TABLE OF CONTENTS will give some idea of its value:

Selections for Albums.—Table of the Principal Alloys.—Ages Attained by Different Animals.—Area and Population of Principal Countries of the World.—Officers of the United States Army and Navy.—Bible Facts.—First Translation of the Bible.—Ages attained by Birds.—Capacity of Boxes.—Notable Bridges of the World.—Facts for Builders.—Capacity of Cisterns and Wells.—Rule for Measuring the Capacity of Circular Cisterns.—Rule for Measuring the Capacity of Square Cisterns.—Climates of the United States.—Coins, Weights and Measures of Scripture.—How to Measure Corn in Cribs when Sides are Flaring.—How to Measure Corn in Cribs when Sides are Straight.—Days of the Week.—Distances by Water from New York to Foreign Ports.—Origin of the Dollar.—Chemical Names for some of the more common Drugs.—Presidential Elections· Popular and Electoral Votes for President and Vice-President of the United States from 1789 to 1880.—Filibuster.—Language of Flowers.—Flying Dutchman.—Digestion of Food.—Food for Stock.—Government of Foreign Countries.—Freezing, Fusing and Boiling Points.—Value of a Ton of Gold and Silver.—Historical Events, Handy Facts and Notable Discoveries.—Legal Holidays of the United States.—Facts Concerning the Hore.—Hints for Housekeepers.—Strength of Ice.—Inks and Paints; how to Mix Printing Inks and Paints in the Preparation of Tints.—Interest Laws in the United States.—First Locomotive used in the United States.—Maine Law.—Miscellaneous Measures.—Time at which Money Doubles at Compound Interest.—Value of Foreign Money in United States Currency.—The Derivations of the Names of the Months.—Number of Nails and Tacks in a Pound.—Depth of the Ocean.—Sizes of Flat Writing Paper.—Origin of the term Penny as applied to Nails.—Peter Funk.—Origin of Plants.—Antidotes for Poison.—Population of 100 Principal Cities of the United States.—Postal Laws.—Food for Poultry.—Language of Precious Stones.—Prices of the Necessaries of Life in the United States and Europe in 1878.—Public Debt of the United States at the close of each Administration.—First Railroads in the United States.—First Appearance of the Rooster in Politics.—Salt River.—Bushels of Seed to the Acre.—Vitality of Seeds.—The Seven Hills of Rome.—The Seven Sleepers.—The Seven Wise Men of Greece.—The Seven Wonders of the World.—Food for Sheep.—Cost of Smoking.—Number of Union Soldiers furnished by each State and Territory during the Rebellion.—Derivation of Names of States and Territories, Fictitious Names, Election Days, Governors' Salaries.—First Steamboat in the United States.—Comparative Strength of Timber and Cast Iron.—Tunnels of the World.—Government of the United States.—Comparative Rate of Weekly Wages Paid in Europe and the United States in 1878.—Cost of the Wars of the United States.—Wedding Anniversaries.—Weight, Avoirdupois, of a Cubic Foot of Different Substances.

The book contains 64 pages, and is handsomely bound in Leatherette, flexible cover.

Mailed, postage prepaid, on receipt of price, 25c., by

RAND, McNALLY & CO., Publishers,

823 Broadway, NEW YORK.   148—154 Monroe St., CHICAGO.

She shivered and moaned, there was such a change in the way Andras pronounced this word, which he had spoken a moment before in tones so loving and caressing,—*Princess.*

Now the word threatened her.

"Listen! I am going to tell you: I wished—Ah! My God! My God! Unhappy woman that I am! Do not read, do not read!"

Andras, who had turned very pale, gently removed her grasp from the package, and said, very slowly and gravely, but with a tenderness in which hope still appeared:

"Come, Marsa, let us see; what do you wish me to think? Why do you wish me not to read these letters? for letters they doubtless are. What have letters sent me by Count Menko to do with you? You do not wish me to read them?"

He paused a moment, and then, while Marsa's eyes implored him with the mute prayer of a person condemned to death by the executioner, he repeated:

"You do not wish me to read them? Well, so be it; I will not read them, but upon one condition: you must swear to me, understand, swear to me, that your name is not traced in these letters, and that Michel Menko has nothing in common with the Princess Zilah."

She listened, she heard him; but Andras wondered if she understood, she stood there so still and motionless, as if stupefied by the shock of a moral tempest.

"There is, I am certain," he continued in the same calm, slow voice, "there is within this envelope, some lie, some plot. I will not even know what it is. I will not ask you a single question, and I will throw these letters,

"Believe me, Sarah, there is a sweeter pleasure than that of vengeance; that of pardon. I do not tell you to forget; I know that one can not command one's heart—but forgive! Remember that there are about you many creatures unhappier than yourself, and concentrate your thoughts on the noble aim of saving so many unfortunates from misery and the cruelty of their lords. Remember——"

"Forgive?" she interrupted bitterly. "At this moment when vengeance is within my grasp, do you know what is my only regret? It is that this vengeance will be insufficient to satisfy the hatred that consumes me!"

"Sarah!"

"Yes, I would like to be able to invent new tortures; I would like to be able to unite in one mass all the sorrows, all the insults I have suffered, in order to crush the Count and his bride, in order to make them suffer in one day what I have suffered all my life! Oh! I would like to trample their hearts under my feet, and read a mortal anguish in each pulsation!"

"For Heaven's sake, Sarah, be calm!"

"Who speaks to me of Heaven?" she cried violently. "I know no longer anything but Hell! I tell you, Florian, the perfidy of the Count and the contempt of my rival have been to me like so much poison poured into my veins. Ah! If this poisoned blood could but fall drop by drop upon the hearts of those who have wronged me!"

As she spoke these words the movement of the lights in the chapel showed that the bridal train was about to leave it.

"The following day she sought an interview with the man whom she, with her husband, had called a friend. She had resolved to sacrifice her own honor, to save that of the man she loved!

"Her husband's debts were paid, and soon after he returned home, but not to happiness, for shortly afterwards his wife died, first confessing to him the sacrifice she had made.

"He took an oath that the man who had thus dishonored him should not go unpunished, and sought a speedy opportunity of revenging himself. They fought, and he believed that he had killed his enemy, but the latter was only wounded, and afterwards swore that his adversary had attempted to murder him. The villain, who was rich, and therefore all-powerful, was believed; and the other, after having witnessed the confiscation of his property, was condemned to exile.

"And now that you have followed me attentively," said the duke de Lorma, "I will make known to you the two men of whom I have been speaking. The one who was exiled was called the count de Merman. The other, the villain who had seduced his wife, was the baron de Vergins, your father!"

A cry of astonishment which Emma could not

Before the eight o'clock train left for the East, Mrs. Baxter sent for her bill, and in half an hour she was speeding over the Lake Shore Railroad, tickets for New York in her pocket. Three days later, I was informed by telegraph from our New York correspondent that she had sailed for Europe in the Germanica.

The reader can not have forgotten the thrill of horror which ran through the country when the news came of the terrible catastrophe in the British Channel, when the Germanica was run down by a heavily-laden merchant vessel, and all on board, with the exception of a few sailors, perished. Among those who found a watery grave were Mrs. Mortimer-Baxter and her maid—the same woman who played the role of the mother of the child on the night that it was first taken from the house on De Puyster street.

* * * * *

On the night of —— I met in the card-room of one of Chicago's fashionable clubs the gentleman who spoke to Garvey on the night of his visit to the —— Hotel. I had gone to the club to hunt up a New York gentleman visiting in the city, and there met Mr. ——. "Oh, by the

there had evidently been threats of a separation. The Congregationalists present looked at their Episcopalian brethren in triumph, as much as to say, "We told you so;" but the latter returned the look with interest, since it was not quite clear who was the wronged person in this connubial tift.

All eyes were turned on Bartel when he was called upon to tell what he knew about the affair. Many of the neighbors had not seen him since he left the town a year before, and they scanned his dull, almost repulsive features, with an eager desire to discover traces of the gay but bloodthirsty Lothario who had played sad havoc with the domestic peace of David Jones, and finally sent the honest farmer hurrying to his last account.

Their scrutiny was by no means satisfactory to the country critics. Dick was morose and sullen, and more than one remarked that the woman who could squander wifely honor for such an ill-favored scoundrel was fitter for a lunatic asylum than an honored niche in Montcalm society.

As he took the oath to tell the truth, and nothing but the truth, Bartel shot a quick, in-

looked in. He was growing quite impatient. I had no reason for wishing to prolong the conversation, so I told him I should have finished in a moment. He nodded his head, and withdrew.

"If there is anything more I can do, let me know," I said, turning to Ceneri.

"There is nothing——Stay! one thing. Macari, that villain—sooner or later he will get his deserts. I have suffered—so will he. When that time comes, will you try to send me word? It may be difficult to do so, and I have no right to ask the favor. But you have interest, and might get intelligence sent me. If I am not dead by then, it will make me happier."

Without waiting for my reply, he walked hastily to the door, and, with the sentry at his side, was marched off to the prison. I followed him.

As the cumbrous lock was being turned, he paused. "Farewell, Mr. Vaughan," he said. "If I have wronged you, I entreat your pardon. We shall meet no more."

"So far as I am concerned, I forgive you freely."

He hesitated a moment, and then held out his hand. The door was now open. I could see the

IN THE RUE DE LA PAIX.

"Yes, do," responded Fedora.

A cab was passing, and Marietta took it. Fedora refused the offer of the concierge to sit down in his room, but walked nervously up and down the sidewalk, glancing every now and then at the closed windows. She saw that the inside blinds were shut, so that the apartments must be in complete darkness. Then her husband could not have arisen. As soon as this thought struck her, she hastened to the concierge and begged him to force the door. The concierge went to fetch a locksmith. In five minutes the latter arrived. At the same moment a carriage turned the corner of the street, drew up before the house, and Marietta alighted.

"Well?" cried Fedora.

Marietta responded by a shake of the head.

Fedora ascended to the entresol with the locksmith.

"You will have a hard time to open it," said the concierge, "there is a bolt and chain, besides the lock."

But, to his great astonishment, the bolt was not drawn, and the door was quickly opened.

Fedora rushed in.

She crossed the antechamber, the dining room and the salon; everything was in its accustomed order.

She entered the bedroom, the door of which was wide open.

Suddenly Marietta heard a cry, a terrible cry. She ran into the room.

Fedora was lying unconscious in the middle of the chamber.

Half on the floor and half on the bed was the body of a man, covered with blood.

And upon a leaf of an open memorandum book, were these words, written in blood:

"Fedora, avenge me. The assassin is—"

over, that Sir Mervyn Ferrand was her husband; that he had ill-used her. She would most certainly know to whom Philippa had fled. It did not follow that because I was ignorant as to who were my neighbors, they knew nothing about me. At any rate, William, my man, would know the truth. So far as I could see, to-morrow or, by the latest, the next day Philippa would be arrested for the crime. Most probably, I should also be included in the arrest. For that I seemed to care nothing; except that it might hinder me from helping my poor girl.

Any hope of removing Philippa—there, put it in plain words—any hope of flight, for days, even weeks, was vain. Let everything go as well as can be in such cases, the girl must be kept in seclusion and quiet for at least a fortnight or three weeks. I groaned as I thought of what would happen if Philippa was arrested and carried before the magistrates, accused of the awful crime. From that moment until the day of her death she would be insane.

Yet, what help was there for it? The moment the deed is known—the moment Mrs. Wilson learns that Sir Mervyn Ferrand has been found shot through the heart, she will let it be known that Lady Ferrand is at hand; and Lady Fer-

THE CHICAGO HERALD

LARGEST MORNING CIRCULATION

IT HAS A BOOM.

READ IT AND LEARN WHY.

IN CHICAGO.

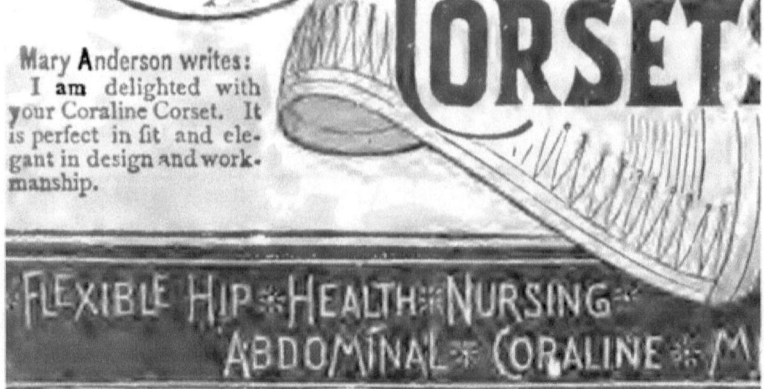

Mary Anderson writes:
I **am** delighted with your Coraline Corset. It is perfect in fit and elegant in design and workmanship.

FLEXIBLE HIP * HEALTH * NURSING * ABDOMINAL * CORALINE * M

Coraline is not Hemp, Jute, Tampico, or Mexican Grass.
Coraline is used in no goods except those sold by WARNER BROTHERS.
The genuine **Coraline** is superior to whalebone, and gives honest perfect satisfaction.
Imitations are **a** fraud and dear at any price.
For sale **by** all leading merchants.   Price from **$1.00** up.

WARNER BROTHERS,
353 BROADWAY, NEW YORK.   257 and 259 STATE STREET,

www.ingramcontent.com/pod-product-compliance
Lightning Source LLC
Chambersburg PA
CBHW030250170426
43202CB00009B/692